DYSPRAXIAS

Jenö Kollarits

and the

Earliest Scientific Study
of Errors of Action

ENGLISH TRANSLATION OF ORIGINAL GERMAN
TEXT

COMMENTARY AND EDITING

BY

JOHN W. SENDERS

For my old friend, Willi Stein

JENÖ KOLLARITS

Contents

JENÖ KOLLARITS

Acknowledgements

My long-time friend, the late Dr. Willi Stein, a scientist of the *Bundesamt fur Sicherheit in the Informationstechnik* (BSI) in Bonn, agreed with me that Kollarits' work is of importance in the history of the study of human error, and has much to contribute to modern theoretical and applied problems. He worked with me on an initial, partial, translation, and made the arrangements for a full translation by the *Bundessprachenamt*, the Language Bureau of the Federal Republic of Germany. I gratefully acknowledge their assistance and the meticulous work of the translator. A policy of that office is that individual translators may not be acknowledged by name.

Dr. Anne Hardy, of the Wellcome Institute for the History of Medicine, put me in touch with Dr. Emese Lafferton of the University of Edinburgh, who, in turn, suggested Dr. Julia Gyimesi of Budapest, who was an invaluable assistant in researching records and personal memories of Kollarits in Budapest and elsewhere in Hungary.

Without the help of number 3 son, Daniel Sellen, I would still be in a state of complete frustration. His ability to find his way through the digital maze involved in preparing a publishable document leads me to wonder wherein I have failed.

Maxine Sidran has been my alter-ego: she edits, corrects, foresees complications, and solves insolvable problems of editing and publishing.

Ann Crichton-Harris has been a constant source of enthusiastic encouragement, a meticulous copy-editor, a searcher for references, a source of sensitive comment and of moral urgency. *Sine uxorem nihil.*

John W. Senders, PhD
Professor Emeritus
Department of Mechanical & Industrial Engineering
Faculty of Applied Science
University of Toronto

Foreword

The twenty-first century has shown an increased interest in the nature of human error, especially in those areas that affect many people in the ordinary course of life. People are especially vulnerable to the consequences of error in medicine and in transportation — almost unavoidable aspects of modern life. One consequence of new medicine is a dramatically increased interest in the effects of failures of both humans and machines to secure the safety of patients. New drugs and devices have been developed with great power to cure, and, if misused, to injure and kill. Similarly, modern transportation systems that move us swiftly and cheaply are also subject to failures, of machines or people, that can have catastrophic results.

Blame is the usual response when a medical accident has happened. We identify a scapegoat (a physician, a nurse, a pharmacist) and punish that person for the unintentional injury. We have tended to assume that 'if only he had done X, or Y or Z', the injury would not have occurred. Therefore the person(s) who failed to do X, or Y or Z, must be held responsible for the injury and liable to pay compensation and be punished. Adverse events that are attributed to human failure can lead to loss of license, a prison term, a fine, and--perhaps most important--public exposure as having been responsible for the pain and suffering of patients and their families.

In the behavioral sciences there has been a gradual shift in the approach to human error. There has been an incremental change from the search for someone or something to blame for error-induced injury to the search for ways to prevent error-induced injury. Error changed from being merely an index of performance, or lack of it, to being the object of study itself. 'How many errors?' was replaced, in part, by 'What exactly was the error?' and 'Why did the error happen?' The first Clambake Conference on the Nature and Source of Human Error in 1980, and the second conference in 1983, were followed by the publication of books, journal articles and dissertations. People began to collect data on errors.

These various works classified errors, created and tested theories of error production, and, depending on the theoretical position of the proponent, proposed ways of reducing their number and their adverse outcomes. A 'science of error' grew. This new science has emerged as a consequence of a paradigm shift--a new way of thinking about errors: error as a natural element of behavior. It was recognized that 'nuclear' errors, 'aviation' errors and 'medical' errors were all the same errors that had not been classified as such in the past by their own characteristics but by the situation in which they had occurred.

There is no ancient history of the science of error: everything is new and, for the most part, computer-searchable.

However, there is a modern history that has escaped the attention of virtually all workers in the field. The contribution of Jenö Kollarits was discovered accidentally in 1981. In the course of a sabbatical year in 1979-1980, a research assistant of the editor noted a reference to a work in German by a Hungarian, J. Kollarits: *Beobachtungen über Dyspraxien (Fehlhandlungen)* in Arkiv der Gesammte Psychologie 1937. There is a copy in the U.S. Library of Congress.

Kollarits had published a diary study of human error. The data were coherent and consistent; the theoretical constructs were reasonable. He saw error as a phenomenon apart from the environment in which it occurs. The outcome of the error is totally dependent on the setting. In other words, the expression of an error, the unintentional action, must be selected from the 'affordances' of the situation.

Kollarits had anticipated much of the modern work on human error. The framework for his interpretation was that of psychiatry, so much of his argument may seem strange to the modern student of error. Nonetheless, he has gained more respect and sympathy for his psychiatric and psychoanalytic models over time.

Kollarits' suggestions for the useful application of his work were modest but in the right direction. When he wrote, there was no engineering psychology, no human factors, and no ergonomics. Nonetheless, his results have been useful in the analysis of both medical and transportation accidents.

Kollarits himself referred to earlier material: *"Schriften zur Fehlerkunde'* (Writings on the Science of Error), a series of papers by Weimer and Kiessling between 1925 and 1929. These will be the subject of further studies.

John W. Senders

Editor's Preface

In 1973 the Office of Scientific Research (OSR) of the United States Air Force (USAF) asked me to report on a meeting in which OSR-supported scientists were to present their progress on the topic of Manual Control Modeling. I was looking forward to this commission, because a number of the presenters I had known personally over the years, and this would be an opportunity to meet then again and all in one place.

They reported on their work for two days. When it was time to make my assessment and offer some commentary, I spoke briefly. I said that I had found all of the work of excellent quality. The experiments were well executed, and the data were properly analyzed. Each contributor was able to report that his model predicted human behavior with 92% to 95% accuracy.

What they could not predict they termed "noise," and by this they meant errors. Error had not been built into their models. I heard myself say: "You are paying attention to the wrong things. You should not waste time in analyzing correct human behaviour. You should pay attention to, and explain, the errors made by the human controllers. It is these errors that destroy materiel, kill personnel, lose battles, and waste money. You should identify the errors and classify them. You should analyze them to discover their causes. Then your work will have even greater value."

When I returned to Canada, I decided to take my own advice. I started looking at human error as an object of scientific study, rather than as aberrant behaviour to be discarded.

John W. Senders

Introduction

This book presents a translation (from the German) of the text of what may be the first diary study of human error.

Jenö Kollarits was born in 1870 and died in 1940. He identifies himself (in this text of 1937) as a tuberculosis patient in a sanatorium. He was probably in the "Kekesteto Hotel and Sanatorium", built in 1932 as the only "modern health hotel" in Matrafüred, in the mountains of Hungary. He also spent time in a sanatorium in the Swiss Alps. The place and nature of his death are unknown to me. Beyond these few notes there seems to be nothing about his life. His papers, on a variety of topics other than error, can be found in Hungarian, French and German journals.

Kollarits carefully points out in the text that he was a tuberculosis patient at the time he collected the errors made by himself and his wife, Anna, who was resident with him at the sanatorium. Whether she was also a patient is not stated, although one can infer from the text that she was. Kollarits discusses at some length his concern that the disease might have an effect on the nature and number of her and his observed errors.

The 1937 paper (a journal article of more than ninety pages!) is a 'diary study' of human error, very much like those of Norman[1] Sellen[2], and Reason[3]. It presents a collection of about 1100 errors and offers a useful taxonomy of error, as well as an attractive, equally useful, theoretical basis for the occurrence of such errors. Kollarits also invents, in passing, the application of error analysis to problems in design for human control of machines. This was an astonishing anticipation of modern ergonomic analysis of system usability and reliability

He was a neurologist and a psychiatrist, but his approach to the investigation of human error was unlike that of Freud and very like that of the great naturalist, botanist and zoologist, Linnaeus (1707-1778), renowned for his taxonomies of plants, animals and minerals.

Kollarits' 1937 work, presented here in translation, was a classic application of the Linnaean model. He observed and collected a corpus of specimen errors of action; noted similarities and differences between and within varieties; and created an economical four-fold taxonomy of such

---

[1] Norman D., *Categorization of Action Slips*. Psychology Review Vol. 88, 1. 1-15, 1981

[2] Sellen, Abigail J., *Mechanisms of Human Error and Human Error Detection*, PhD dissertation, U C San Diego, 1990

[3] Reason, J. and K. Mycielska, *Absent-minded? The Psychology of Mental Lapses and Everyday Errors*, Prentice Hall Inc., Inglewood Cliffs, NJ, 1982

errors: substitution, repetition, omission and insertion. He then theorized on the mechanisms that might give rise to the varieties and proposed general laws that he thought facilitated the production of each kind of error. He found that a great majority, about two thirds, of errors were substitution. He attributed these to assimilation based on similarity, a concept that underlies much modern work, especially that aimed at confusion between medications.

He proposed that underlying all error was the 'Principle of Least Effort'. This brilliant insight leads to a simple solution to what might otherwise be difficult, sometimes intransigent, problems of design. In short, the easier it is to do the wrong thing, the more likely it is to be done. In passing, almost as a throw-away line, he conceived and described what is now called Ergonomics or Human Factors as a principle of design for efficient and reliable human performance in the control of complex systems.

Jeno Kollarits should have been famous. He presented the first logical theory of human error; he invented the concept of ergonomic design; he proposed rational theoretical causal mechanisms of human error.

At the time of Linnaeus' death in 1778, he was known throughout Europe. At the time of Kollarits' death in 1940, he and his work were virtually unknown. This major error paper is not cited in any modern writing.

This was probably due to unfortunate timing--the outbreak of World War Two. Further, the fact that this work had been published in German would have made it invisible to most English-speaking scientists.

Jeno Kollarits was a contemporary of Sigmund Freud (1856-1939). Both men thought about and wrote about error, but in totally different ways. It is instructive to contrast their explanations of why errors occur.

Freud appears to have been the first to publish a psychological theory of error. He based his analysis on a set of hypothetical functional structures of the human mind--the psychoanalytic model. His theories were immensely popular with non-scientific readers; the concepts he created are deeply embedded in modern thought and language.

Freud's major discussion of error appeared in 1901 in *The Psychopathology of Everyday Life,* wherein he set out a theory that attributed virtually all errors to mechanisms in the 'unconscious'. The following is a typical example of Freud's causal analysis.

In the chapter on error, Freud states: (Brill's translation of 1914): "In my book, "The Interpretation of Dreams", I was responsible for a series of errors in historical and, above all, in material facts, which I was astonished to discover after the appearance of the book. On closer examination, I found that they did not originate from my ignorance but could be traced to errors of memory explainable by means of analysis. On page 361 I indicated as Schiller's birthplace the city of Marburg, a name which recurs in Styria. The error is found in the analysis of a dream during a night journey, from which I was awakened by the conductor calling out the name of the station, Marburg. In the contents of the dream, inquiry is made concerning a book by Schiller. But Schiller was not born in the university town of Marburg, but in the Swabian city Marbach. I maintain that I always knew this."

The attribution of his error to unconscious mechanisms and dreams is unconvincing. Freud's failure even to mention the obvious similarity of the two names as a possible basis for the error is astonishing.

Kollarits would have identified the offering of an incorrect name, Marburg, as Schiller's birthplace, to be an 'Error of Substitution'. And, more importantly, Kollarits would have attributed it to the similarity between the two names Marburg and Marbac, as we would today when analyzing drug-substitution errors that occur frequently in medicine.

Some modern studies of error consider errors in different settings to be inherently different errors. Thus a medication error of substitution of one drug for another would be considered to be unrelated to the substitution of one automobile control for another. The effects are, of course, different, but the underlying mechanism is very likely to be the same for the two very different-appearing errors. Kollarits' analysis makes it clear that an error may be expressed in different ways as a function of its setting, but that the form of the error is independent of the setting.

Many of the daily activities that are described in the paper may sound a bit odd to the modern reader. However, there really was a time, only seventy years ago, when people used inkwells and dipped pens into them to make marks on paper.

John W. Senders

COMPLETE ENGLISH TEXT

Observations on Dyspraxias (Errors of Action)
Comparing Errors in Speaking, Reading and Writing
(Homogeneous attraction and inhibition; suppression of
differences; commenced melody; entirety and elements; typological
comments)
by
Jenö Kollarits, Budapest
presently in Mátrafüred (Hungary)
(with 4 tables in the text)

1 Introduction

This publication is a continuation of my work on errors in speaking, writing and reading, on assimilation, on Ranschburg's "homogeneous inhibition and homogeneous attraction," and on the recognition and suppression of differences.[45] It presents and analyses a collection of 1100 errors which can

---

[4] "Sur les images visuelles qui accompagnent la représentation des individus et des lieux inconnus," *Archives de Psychologie*, 14 (1914). - "Die Rolle der Assimilation bei Vorstelungen vom Unbekannten," *Journ. f. Psychol. u. Neurol.*, 23 (1918). - "Über Traumassimilation," Ibid., 23 (1918). - "Über Assimilationen von Personenvorstellungen," Ibid., 23 (1918). - "Zuhilfenahme der Visualisation bei physiol. und pathol. Erinnerungslücken, besonders von Namen und Zahlen," *Zeitschr. f. ges. Neurol. Psychiatrie*, 54 (1920). - "Eine psychiatr. Untersuchungsmethode: Die Erkennung des Differenten," *Arch. f. Psychiatrie*, 85 (1928). - "Über Verschmelzung und Assimilation. Das Gesetz der angeschlagenen Melodie und des angeschlagenen Akkordes," *Ranschburg-Festschrift*, 1929. - "Über Akzentlegasthenie und disjunktive Legasthenie im allg. und als kl. Zeichen der Geistesschwächung bei Tbc. und im Alter. Das Verhältnis zwischen der inneren Sprache und Schreibfehler. Homogene Hemmung u. Unterdrückung des Differenten," *Arch. f. Psychiat.*, 99 (1933). - "Die Verschiedenheit der Ichstörung der Traumsprache, der hypnagogen Halluzinationen und der Schizophrenie. Charakter-, Prozeß- und biologische Halluzinationen. Gespräche mit Schlafenden. Homogene Hemmung, Einschaltung und Unterdrückung des Differenten. Gesetz der angeschlagenen Melodie u. des angeschlagenen Akkordes," Ibid., 101 (1933). -"Beobachtungen über Lesefehler bei stummen Lesen mit einer Bemerkung über Titeln und Annoncen. (RANSCHBURGsche Hemmung. Homogene Attraktion. Unterdrückung des Differenten. Gesetz der angeschlagenen Melodie.)," *Dieses Arch*, 95 (1935).
[5] Greene, R.L.; "The Ranschburg effect: the role of guessing strategies. "The Ranschburg effect refers to the finding of impaired serial recall of items repeated on a list. One account attributes this effect to the use of a strategy where subjects avoid using as guesses stimuli that they had recalled elsewhere on the list. Support for this interpretation is reported here. The Ranschburg effect is eliminated when subjects

be compared with errors in speaking, reading and writing, errors in the assimilation of ideas in a waking or hypnagogic state, and which, based on neurological and psychiatric terminology, can be called 'dyspraxias' or action errors.

Of the 1,100 such errors I was able to collect over a period of 10 months, 664 are my own, 417 are my wife's, and 19 were made by seven people who live close to me and who committed errors in my presence. I did not have a large number of experimental subjects at my disposal. In addition to this collection, further observations of errors made by ourselves and by others were known to me before beginning and after my completing the collection. These observations confirmed the findings of the series but did not tell us anything new. The agreement between the two larger series (664 and 417), along with what we know about errors in speaking, reading and writing, confirm the conclusions drawn from the observations. Extending the study to cover a larger number of persons could, however, bring to light further valuable details about individual differences in the science of action errors.

My material comprises a series with some limits with respect to completeness. This is due to the fact that errors of action are spread amongst the actions of everyday life, are difficult to remember on account of their fleeting nature, or are hardly noticed at all. When an action is carried out, attention is paid to its purpose and not to the error and its concomitants. Cases that could not be remembered in precise detail were removed from the series. This could not have an influence on the results of the study. On the contrary, partially forgotten errors may very well be importantly different from those that were well recalled.

I have included in the collection both errors completed and errors that started but intercepted. A completed error is, for example, when I dip my pen into my tea cup instead of into the ink pot beside it. An interrupted error, by contrast, is when I am about to dip my pencil instead of my pen into the ink pot, realize what I am doing, and discontinue the action. Whether only begun or completed, they are both errors and, indeed, substitution errors.

I attempted to study interrupted and completed errors separately, but soon gave up this approach, since differentiation was not always possible or depended solely on external circumstances. If, for example, I go into my room in the middle of the day and reach for the light switch as I am accustomed to do when there is little natural light, it is of little importance for our study whether I turn on the lights, only touch the light switch, or merely raise my hand to do so. Whether the error in this case is interrupted

are instructed to avoid guessing. Also, the Ranschburg effect is found in partial report only when subjects are told that the crucial item occurred elsewhere on the list." Mem Cognit. 1991 May;19(3):313-7.

or completed can point towards a difference in the degree of absent mindedness or can depend on the speed of the movement but does not indicate a fundamental difference in the type of error or the conditions required for its emergence. In comparing omissions and substitutions we find the additional problem that omissions cannot merely be commenced; the first wrong movement leads to the termination of the entire action. From other points of view, there are differences between interrupted and completed errors that tell us about the pathology of the subject. In such cases it is important whether the housewife making an omelette mistakenly reaches first for the eggs instead of the butter but recognizes the mistake immediately or whether the aphasic chef Pierre Maries makes the same dish by first cracking the eggs into the pan and only later adding the butter and fails to realize his mistake even when he sees the unsuccessful finished product.

Since the two large series of my collection are based on observations of two patients suffering from *tuberculosis* with *subfebrile body temperatures* and with *tachycardia*, the question must be asked as to the effects of the illness on the data. The answer to this is that the illness influences the *frequency of the errors*, as was the case with errors in speaking, reading and writing. This was shown by the fact that errors increased every time the condition worsened but decreased when the illness subsided. Tuberculosis had no effect on the structure of the errors. It is also unimportant as to which kind of illness is involved. Gaps in one's memory, difficulties in recalling words, especially names and numbers, substitutions, omissions and insertions are frequently found in connection with other illnesses such as, for example, inflammation of the gall bladder, about which I have reported. Wiersma found extended reaction times in *cancer* patients. Tuberculosis entails a poisoning of the cerebral cortex by toxins, poor blood supply to the brain if cardiasthenia and tachycardia are diagnosed, and carbonic acid poisoning if the patient has difficulty breathing. Tuberculosis can also lead to psychological disturbances[6] irritation, absent-mindedness and nervousness lead to a high incidence of these types of errors in healthy persons with respect not only to practice but also to errors in reading and writing that people make every day.

---

[6] For literature on this subject see *Arch. f. Psychiat.*, 99.

2 Statistics on Substitutions, Omissions and Insertions in My Collection

Table 1 presents statistics on substitutions, omissions, insertions and repetitions in my collection of errors. It clearly shows that *substitutions* are *by far most common*, comprising approximately two thirds of all action errors. In terms of frequency, it is followed by omissions with 18.72%, insertions with 12.09% and repetitions with 1.73%. The necessity of treating these percentages as rough figures is clearly evident given the various differences between the two large series, with substitutions varying between 66% and 70% and omissions between 21% and 15%.

Table 1. Statistics on types of error

Forms of error	Subject J.		Subject A.		7 other subjects		All subjects together	
	#	%	#	%	#	%	#	%
Substitutions	436	65.6	293	70.4	13	68.4	742	67.4
Omissions	138	20.7	64	15.4	4	21.3	2016	18.7
Insertions	83	12.5	49	11.8	1	5.3	133	12.1
Repetitions	8	1.2	10	2.4	1	5.3	19	1.73
Total	665	100.0	416	100.0	19	100.0	1100	100.0

In other words, what is important are the large differences and the rank ordering of the frequency, thus: substitutions, omissions, insertions and repetitions. Upon further inspection, we can also see that Hermann Weimer[7] was correct in considering the classes of substitutions, omissions and 'supplements' (what I call 'insertions' and 'repetitions') to be mere *forms*

---

[7] H. Weimer, *Psycholgie der Fehler*, Leipzig: Klinkhardt, 1929, 2nd Ed.

and not *types of error*. We should not overlook the fact that many omissions can, to a certain extent, be considered substitutions. If, for example (case 60), someone getting dressed reached for his socks before putting on his long underwear, the lower sections of which belong under the long socks, he omitted to put on his long underwear, the lower sections of which belong under the long socks, he omitted to put on his long underwear, but, at the same time, substituted the two above-mentioned long socks. In case 7, by contrast, in which someone forgot to close doors, we cannot speak of a substitution, the reason being that this omission has nothing to do with the following action, namely going onto the veranda.

If someone has to lay a series of blankets, quilts and pillows on a bed in a prescribed order, omits the middle item, for example the gray blanket, and reaches for the blue blanket instead, this person will have committed an omission but, at the same time, will have mistakenly substituted the blue blanket for the gray. If, on the other hand, the last item of the series belonging on the bed is omitted, and the next action leads one into the kitchen, we cannot claim that making and lighting a fire has been substituted for the placing of a decorative pillow on the bed. Omitting an action in the middle of a homogeneous series of actions, such as getting dressed, shaving with a safety razor, or making a bed, is also a substitution, whereas the same action, if it is the last element in a series, is not a substitution. I have classified these cases as omissions, since that is primarily what I see in them. Another reason for such an approach is that in reading, speaking and writing, any omission of a word, syllable or letter or, in writing, part of a letter (with the exception of the last word or letter of the entire material being handled) could be interpreted as a substitution.

The question must also be asked as to whether the *differences* in percentages of forms of error depend on *personal idiosyncrasies*. This is possible but cannot be answered with the help my collection. On the other hand, it could be that the differences resulted from the material; in other words that the everyday things one person does are different from those of another and thus some forms of error could have more opportunities to occur than others.

Table 2 compares *the findings of my current study* with those of my earlier studies on *errors in reading, errors in internal speaking, i.e. the self-dictation which precedes meaningful writing*, as well as errors in *speaking in a hypnagogic state, and errors in writing* based on correct and incorrect self-dictation of meaningful writing.

Table 2. Comparison of action errors with errors in reading, speaking, and writing examined in my earlier studies.

		Forms of error											
		Disjun		Substit		Omiss		Insert		Repet			
		#	%	#	%	#	%	#	%	#	%	#	%
Errors		-	-	742	67	206	19	133	12	19	2		100
Read	Sent	19	100									19	100
	Word	16	2	728	84	102	2	22	2	1	0	87	100
	Syllable	-	-	-	-	10	-	-	-	-	-	10	100
	Letter	-	-	16	42	14	37	6	16	2	5	38	100
	Total	35	37	744	75	126	14	28	3	3	0	936	100
Speak	Sent	-	-	132	92	3	2	1	1	7	5	143	100
	Word	-	-	1	14	6	86	-	-	-	-	7	100
	Syllable	-	-	10	59	2	12	5	29	-	-	17	100
	Letter	-	-	15	84	3	17	-	-	-	-	18	100
	Total	-	-	158	85	14	8	6	3	7	4	185	100
Errors	Sent	-	-	3	75	1	25	-	-	-	-	4	100
	Word	-	-	82	75	18	16	9	8	1	1	110	100
	Letter	-	-	10	63	-	-	6	37	-	-	16	100
	Total	-	-	93	73	19	15	15	12	1	1	130	100
Errors	Sent	-	-	75	96	2	3	-	-	1	1	78	100
	Word	-	-	-	-	2	-	-	-	-	-	2	100
	Syllable	-	-	6	60	1	10	3	30	-	-	10	100
	Letter	-	-	10	59	7	41	-	-	-	-	17	100
	Total	-	-	91	85	12	11	3	3	1	1	107	100
Errors	Sent	-	-	4	33	5	42	-	-	3	25	12	100
	Word	-	-	-	-	2	-	-	-	-	-	2	100
	Syllable	-	-	205	49	172	41	19	4	27	6	423	100
	Whole Letter	-	-	3	2	99	83	17	14	1	1	120	100
	Whole, Partial Letter	-	-	208	3	271	50	36	7	28	5	543	100
	Numb	-	-	30	51	22	38	1	2	5	9	58	100
	Total	-	-	242	39	300	49	37	6	36	5.8	615	100
Total errors in writing		-	-	333	46	312	43	40	6	37	5.4	7.22	100
Total errors		35	1.14	2072	67	677	22	222	7	67	2.2	3037	100

Error of internality of the lamp went unnoticed and became suppressed, but that of the pot, which is dissimilar in itself, became suppressed by the lamp which is dissimilar in itself. Apart from the similarity attraction of the pot, which started the error, the dissimilarity-based distraction developed as a second process. The two cases 871 and 199, where the object and its location were subjected to a dissimilarity-based substitution, have already been discussed in detail under the aspect of distraction. As far as the aspect of the suppression of differences is concerned it has to be added that here distraction and the suppression of differences were also a primary and not a secondary aftereffect of a similar inhibition. We do not want to repeat the details of these two cases. The same reflections apply to cases 627, 908, 472 where three dissimilar elements were mistaken for one another. In case 627 the dissimilar wasp suffered death due to the fact that it had distracted the person from carrying away the sheet of lined paper; in case 908 the darkness of the room resulted in a substitution of a completely dissimilar action for the intended one, and in case 472 the opening of the window distracted the person from the intended action of putting down the button. Since these action substitutions did not include any similar element the abstraction and also the suppression of differences must be rated as a primary process that is completely independent of any similarity. That the dissimilarity-based abstraction = distraction is a generally known phenomenon which is of biological importance. It need not always entail dyspraxia. This can be illustrated by an everyday event. I am sitting in front of my writing table and doing some paper work, my wife is sitting at my side and is doing needlework.

(The comparison of writing based on correct and incorrect self-dictation is, however, subject to the restrictions that the retrospective observation of these fleeting phenomena entails difficulties, and that, as a result, some less conspicuous errors of the silent self-dictation easily go unnoticed. These unavoidable shortcomings of introspection, however, do not invalidate the findings.)

The data in the second table are highly dependent on the percentages of the various forms of error from action, speaking, reading and writing. If we add together all errors of action, speaking, reading and writing, we arrive at 3,073 cases, of which, like the collection of action errors, two-thirds are substitutions. Given the possibility of large fluctuations, the fact that omissions comprise 18.73% of action errors and 22.03% of all errors is of little significance. Furthermore, since insertions are 12.09% of action errors and 7.22% of all errors, and repetitions are 1.73% of action errors and 2.18% of all errors, what is important is the order of the figures according to decreasing size: 1. substitutions, 2. omissions, 3. insertions and 4. repetitions.

If we compare the percentages of the various materials of this table with one another, we will find in *reading and speaking errors* the same *preponderance of substitutions over omissions and the aforementioned order of forms of error*. In writing errors, however, omissions are most common as a result of the omission of partial letters. Here omissions amount to 82.50% as opposed to substitutions, which are 2.50%. If we examine in my collection of reading, writing and speaking errors the word, syllable and letter errors on their own (a statistical evaluation is not possible for the 7 syllable errors of internal speech and the 12 word errors of writing), we will note great differences in percentages as shown in the table. Substitutions, for example, range from 96.15 to 42.11%.

Thus, neither the above-mentioned order of frequency nor a strong preponderance of substitutions can be a generally valid law for every series of errors. A higher law must be at work here to which the differences comply. This law, which is psychological, physiological and biological and which can even be found in the so-called inorganic world, is the Hamiltonian *principle of least resistance* or, what amounts to the same, the principle of least effort. Depending on material and person, the least effort must find various paths of least resistance.

Despite the 3,073 cases in my collection, the figures for some materials and forms of error are still too small for us to draw final conclusions. Further material must be collected for these sorts and forms of error, e.g. on letter errors in reading, of which my collection only has 38 cases from a total of 1,000 errors in reading, or on errors in the internal speaking of numbers, of which I have a mere 18 cases, or on syllable errors in writing, of which I could find only four.

The Hamiltonian principle of least resistance is seen, on the one hand, in *errors in reading* by the fact that *larger complexes* offer *more resistance* to errors than do smaller ones. This is why, for example, 91.63% of word substitutions refer to one word and only 8.37% refer to several words. On the other hand, the above-mentioned order of error forms appears at least in part to derive from the fact that one form requires more effort than the others if other conditions are influencing it as well. For example, if there are more possibilities for one form than for another.[8] In this matter, however, the conditions are not clear in all respects. In general we can say that *the more infrequent an error, the more difficult it must be for this error to occur* and the larger it must be. If, however, omissions are in general more serious errors than substitutions, the substitution of an important word is, in its practical consequences and perhaps even from a psychological viewpoint, a more serious error than the omission of an unimportant word.

The practical consequences must be considered separately. Saying "right" instead of "left," for example, is a substitution on account of the

---

[8] For further information, see my study published in *Arch f. d. ges. Psychol.*, 95.

parallel identity of the opposed terms, since both words refer to a direction. From a psychological point of view, this error is not particularly serious and can easily be corrected in everyday conversations. When, however, an English captain commanded his vessel to proceed at full steam in the wrong direction and ran aground, the ship and every living creature aboard perished.

If a cashier were to write 6 instead of 9 on account of their parallel identity, the error is of little importance if the difference is only 3 pfennigs but of major importance if it is RM 300 000. From a purely psychological point of view, however, the errors are the same or practically the same, although the cashier should have paid more attention in the latter case.

The Hamiltonian *principle* also applies to the *action* errors in our present collection. Here, as well, we can also say that actions in general offer the least resistance against substitutions, more against omissions, more still against insertions and most against repetitions, or, in other words, that, in general, from a purely psychological perspective, substitutions are the least serious errors and insertions and repetitions the most serious, with the substitution of an important action being at least as serious from a practical and psychological point of view as an unimportant erroneous insertion. With respect to this "hierarchy," a further object of study would be to determine whether some everyday actions such reading, writing and speaking provide more opportunities for the development of one form of error than for others.

3 Substitutions

Actions can involve substitutions of:

1. the objects one grasps, looks for, searches or strives for;
2. the places where one goes, where one carries or puts something or where one looks for something;
3. the activity one uses at the right place and with the right objects;
4. the combinations of objects, places and activities.

   1. *Examples of object substitutions*: J. Picks up the inkwell instead of the teacup next to it (no. 11); takes to the medicine cupboard the pocket watch instead of the package of quinine powder lying beside it on the table (no. 22); takes off glasses instead of hat upon entering the room (no. 47); instead of taking the gloves on the table, J. reaches for the key to the cupboard in which they are often kept (no. 51).
   2. *Examples of place substitutions*: J. carries waste paper, which is to be burnt, into the bedroom instead of the kitchen (no. 6); dips the pen into the teacup instead of into the adjacent inkpot (no. 9); looks for cotton batting in the clothes closet instead of in the washstand drawer (no. 13); places the lid to the dirty water pail on the washstand pitcher instead of on the pail (no. 24).
   3. *Examples of movement substitutions involving the correct objects at the correct place*: J. tries to open the window by moving the window catch in the wrong direction (no. 26); closes a bolt instead of opening it, because it was open (no. 32); instead of closing an open door, opens it wider (no. 41); pulls a necktie reversed through a pulldown collar (no. 68); pulls the door to the veranda, which opens outwards, instead of pushing it (no. 214).
   4. *Examples of combined substitutions -- object and place substitutions*: instead

of taking the blotting paper from the drawer, J. takes his watch from his vest pocket (no. 21); instead of looking at the thermometer on the wall, J. stares at the picture of Christ on the wall (no. 8); -- *object + movement substitutions*: instead of pulling open the window, J. turns the window catch (no. 28); instead of taking off his hat, J. takes off his glasses (no. 189); -- *place + movement substitutions*: instead of tying his tie in front of the mirror, J. looks out the window (no. 209); instead of taking the dirty water pail to the garden, J. places it in the washbasin on the washstand (no. 259); -- *object + place + movement substitutions*: instead of placing a button on the washstand, J. opens the window (no. 472); A. removes the insole from her shoe instead of taking off her socks (no. 1049).

Table 3 presents statistics on the object, place and movement substitutions, as well as on the combined substitutions in my collection. With respect to the two main subjects, it shows a regularity insofar as *place substitution is most frequent for both and is followed by object substitution, whereas movement substitution involving correct objects in correct places is least frequent*. The 13 errors of the seven other subjects indicate a different type of behavior, since external circumstances favor a certain type of error. Most of these errors involve opening a door to the veranda which opens outwards. Even frequent visitors always attempt to pull it, since almost all doors open inwards. I have thus separately added together the substitutions of the two main test persons.

Table 3: Statistics of object (O), place (P) and movement (M) substitutions and their combinations.

Forms	Subject J.		Subject A.		Subjects J. & A.		7 other subjects		All subjects together	
	#	%	#	%	#	%	#	%	#	%
O	132	31	113	39	245	34	2	15	247	33
P	232	53	152	52	384	33	2	15	386	52
M	50	11	16	5	66	9	9	69	75	10
O&P	6	1	3	1	9	1	-	-	9	1
O&M	5	1	7	2	12	2	-	-	12	2
P&M	3	1	1	0.3	4	1	-	-	4	1
O&P&M	8	2	1	0.3	9	1	-	-	9	1
Total	436	100	293	100	729	100	13	100	742	100

In accordance with the Hamiltonian principle, we can thus assert that in my cases the object offered more resistance to substitutions than did the place, while movement substitutions involving the right object and at the right place offered the greatest resistance. Perhaps there is less opportunity to commit the last form of error. The fact that *combined substitutions are the most infrequent* corresponds with the Hamiltonian principle, since resistance in these cases must, in theory, be *double or triple depending on the number of elements substituted.* The combination of a place substitution with an object substitution should reduce the number of cases to half of the object substitutions or, more precisely, to half of the average of both forms of substitution. This, of course, is by far not the case. The percentage of object substitutions of the two main subjects (33.61) and their place substitutions (52.67) has an average of 43.14%, half of which is 21.57%. Taken as a percentage, this figure should represent double resistance. However, the actual percentage of object and place substitutions is 1.23%, more than 17 times smaller than the above figure. The object substitutions of the two main subjects (33.6%) and their movement substitutions (9.05%) have an average of 21.33%, half of which is 10.66%. The actual percentage of combinations of both substitutions (1.65%) is one sixth as large.

The sum of the percentages of place and movement substitutions is 61.72%, with the average being 30.86% and half of the average being 15.43%. However, the actual percentage of the combination of place and movement substitutions (0.55%) is one twenty-eighth as large as 15.47%. When added together, the percentages of the three forms of substitution give us 95.33%, on average 31.78%, a third of which is 10.59%. By contrast, the combination of the three forms of error (1.23%) is one ninth as large.

The combinations thus surpass the theoretical resistance of the sums of their elements by 17, 6, 28, and 8.5 times. The large differences in these figures should make us suspicious and prevent us from accepting them as absolute quantities. They appear to be dependent on a number of moments which cannot be observed and, insofar as combinations are concerned, to be subject to *the error of small numbers,* since we are dealing here with 9, 12, 4 and 9, in total 34, combined substitutions. This circumstance should also prevent us from using statistics to evaluate the various combinations in relation to one another. Despite all of these drawbacks, we can still say that combinations of objects, places and movements offer considerably more resistance to substitutions than does the sum of their individual components. One could be inclined to conclude that *the process exceeds the purely mechanical in inorganic-physical terms.* This would speak against the application of pure physical mechanics in psychological life and for the paramount importance of biological-psychological work.

I was unable to find data for *a comparison with physics.* The ability of alloys made from several metals to resist tension, pressure and flexion, which would serve as a good comparison here, depends not only on the components of the alloy but also on a number of external circumstances, e.g. heat treatment and other processing methods. The tensile strength of carbon steel (e.g. iron containing 0.6% carbon) which is slowly cooled from 850°C is approximately 55 to 60 kg/mm. When cooled quickly, its tensile strength is between 150 and 200 kg/mm. The tensile strength of pure iron is 30 to 32 kg/mm, while that of carbon can hardly be measured. When an alloy is created out of the two elements, the tensile strength increases, at first considerably, as a result of the added carbon. It later drops below the tensile strength of iron. In some cases, if a strong element is added to a strong alloy, the tensile strength of the new alloy can drop significantly, for example if bronze is added to aluminum. The strength of the substances depends on their crystal structure, which in turn depends on heat treatment and other processing methods. It is even more difficult to draw a comparison with other compounds, since, for example, the concrete in reinforced concrete cracks before the iron does.

With these engineering examples in mind, we can understand just how complicated resistance is in the nervous system, for example when it comes to the reflexes in the switches of the actions and even more so in the human psyche. At present, we are lacking a sufficient basis for clear insights into these phenomena. When it comes to psychological resistance, we may consider the resistance of switches, as in the case of reflexes, but also holistic psychological factors, since the combinations of object, place and movement substitutions comprise entities which signify something completely different from their elements, which can only be artificially observed as separate elements for the purposes of the study. What is important is not only that the entity of the action is something different from the sum of its elements, but also that the substitution does not exist outside the action. The same person who, when writing, dipped his pen in the teacup instead of the inkpot would not confuse the inkpot with the teacup if he merely looked at these two objects outside of this action.

Actions can also be observed from *the same theoretical point of view as language*, since language is also an activity. From this perspective, we can examine actions as *sentences* in which the *active person* is the *subject*, the *action* is the *predicate*, and the *object grasped* and the place to which or from which the action is directed are the *attributes of the predicate*. Given the action errors encountered in everyday life, a substitution of the active person cannot occur even if we assume that the person is healthy and wide awake. The pathological cases of so-called depersonalization and the related phenomena of substitution do not belong to our field of study.

Since the fact of the action is found not only in the subject but also in the predicate with its attributes, we can say that the *predicate of the action sentence offers more resistance to substitutions than do attributes*. This corresponds to the paramount importance of the predicate in a sentence as opposed to that of attributes; a sentence without a predicate is not possible, whereas a sentence can exist without attributes. (I live, I scream and I sing are, for example, sentences without attributes. The happy exclamation of the skier, "Snow!", appears to be without a predicate, but, in fact, means "There is snow" or "It is snowing" and thus contains an unspoken predicate.)

I believe in the sentence character of human error, despite the fact that most are not formulated in words. I reach for the pen without saying, "I am reaching for the pen." Our action sentences are thus at the same time examples of connections of psychological contents without words - "songs without words" - which is not to say that contrary behavior cannot occur as a means of supporting the action. This occurs, in fact, even when abstract thinking is not involved and can be seen especially in complicated and important actions. For example, I know a laryngologist who always said out loud what he intended to do when performing minor nose surgery.

Let us now look at *the conditions which lead to substitutions* (as well as to other human errors). The most important conditions we will come across are those in the subject. If we assume that the subject is in good psychological health, there is no need to doubt the correctness of the intention, as is also the case with slips of the tongue and pen. If I am sitting in front of a bowl of soup, do not have a spoon, and, after recognizing this absence, mistakenly ask for a fork, then I did not mean a fork, but rather a spoon. In the same way, when I dip my pen into my teacup instead of into the inkpot beside it, my intention is to wet my pen with ink, not with tea.

The error, in other words, is not committed by the will but rather at a stage related (not neurologically) but subordinate to the will, namely the stage where the organization of actions is conducted, for the errors of the will, which belong in another category, are ruled out by definition.

In our cases, this can be expressed as follows: *the action is split away from the intention.* This separation is caused by the fact that insufficient attention is paid to the action being carried out. One fails to devote one's full attention to the matter at hand. If, for example, I come across an important point in an article and wish to make a note of it, it can happen that I am so tied up in the article that I have no psychological energy left to correctly move my hand holding the pen to the ink and to take pains to differentiate between teacup and inkpot and where they are standing. In this state I may also fail to recognize the visual and tactile differences between pen and pencil and may take the latter and dip it instead of the pen into the ink. I may even make notes with the pencil, although I should know, if I thought about it, that after a period of some months my notes would be unreadable.

When, immersed in my work, I leave my desk in order to let fresh air into the room, it can happen that I go to the window and grasp the window catch without realizing that it is open. I then attempt to turn it in the only possible direction, i.e. that which closes the window, and shake it angrily without understanding why the window does not give way.

A physiological explanation for the fact that insufficient energy is available for properly carrying out the intended action as a result of concentration on a certain object is given by Ranschburg and called "distributive inhibition." According to this theory, the amount of oxygen available in the arterial blood can only supply a limited number of nerve elements to which it is directed by the cerebral vasomotoric center, which is superior to the oblongata center, as a result of reflecting regulation (experiments of E. Weber). In addition to Ranschburg's distributive inhibition, there appear in certain cases to be other phenomena also related to insufficient oxygen supply. Breathing ceases or becomes shallow during intense mental activity and even concentration.

Jendràssik made us, his students, aware of the fact that his assistants temporarily stopped breathing when they were paying attention to his instructions or explanations. Longer periods of intense concentration or attention can thus lead to inadequate breathing, which, after long periods of irregularity, reduces the amount of oxygen available, thus causing the cortical brain cells to suffer and become exhausted more quickly. That the oxygen supply of the blood actually does decrease after longer periods of intense mental activity is shown by the fact that *yawning*, which has nothing to do with boredom, *automatically* sets in and thus remedies the lack of oxygen by forcing the subject to inhale deeply. (Even boredom leads to shallow breathing and thus, for the same reason, to yawning.)

In illnesses involving labored breathing or poor cardiac activity, the amount of oxygen in the blood and thus the supply to the cerebral cortex is already insufficient prior to distributive inhibition, which thus appears even earlier. In addition, the cerebral cortex can be damaged by poisons such as tuberculosis toxin or cancer toxin, thus making distributive inhibition appear at an earlier stage.

We have already mentioned the separation of the subject from the particulars of the action being carried out. This disorder is one of intention. That being true, we must add action errors to a comprehensive group of psychological phenomena which all belong to intention disorders and thus have some common characteristics.

The term "separation" draws our attention to schizophrenia, i.e. to split personalities. In my opinion schizophrenia is an incorrect name, since, besides splitting, there are completely different and more important symptoms in which, however, split personalities may also play a role. Ego disorders of psychological intention, for example of speaking, also occur in *dreams and hypnagogic hallucinations*. A summary based on common characteristics can shed light on some things but can be dangerous if differences are neglected. For example, several researchers have mistakenly attempted to explain schizophrenia based on dream and hypnagogic experiences, because intention is erroneous in these cases. The mistakes of intention found in dream experiences and hypnagogic states, not only in the errors of healthy subjects, but also in schizophrenia, are different in all of the cases specified. If, when falling asleep, we experience optical and acoustic "hypnagogic" hallucinations, then we have completely given up intention and are "passively" hearing "voices," which we feel to be foreign or "from without" vis-à-vis our ego. Küppers[9] refers to this as ego elimination. After we have passed from the hypnagogic state to dreams, we no longer experience a pure and complete ego elimination, since the ego of dreams is not a passive observer of hallucinations but rather plays an active role in events.

"In the hypnagogic state," I have written,[10] "I am conscious that I am lying in bed and hearing voices. In dreams, I *walk, fly and speak* and I know that I am doing things, that I am speaking, if I can be a passive observer of dream experiences." Leroy[11] is correct in saying that the dreamer takes part in his dream, while the hypnagogic hallucinator merely experiences, but does not play an active role: "Dreams are an adventure, hypnagogic hallucinations are merely an observation."

In other words, dreams are no longer a deficiency as a result of ego elimination, which Küppers mentions, but rather are at least in part an active process which diverges from the normal activities conducted when people are awake. Dreams are a dysfunction. If schizophrenia is also an ego disorder, then this ego disorder is identical to neither that of the hypnagogic state nor that of dreams. It is true that the ego disorder of schizophrenia is in part a deficiency, for example, when afflicted persons passively hear voices. At the same time, however, it is something different, since it creates a delusion unlike that of dreams, and since it shows actively desired peculiarities in speech and eccentricity in body movements (Gruhle[12]) which are done once and then not repeated and which do not occur in dreams. In addition, as Gruhle writes, the consciousness of the dreamer is dulled while that of the schizophrenic is clear. In the hypnagogic state (post-sleep state), the situation is completely different, since this state strives toward awakening.

Following this discussion, we can now turn to ego disorders in errors of action, speaking, writing and reading. Here this disorder is once again different. It is true that we say that absent-mindedness is "like being lost in a dream," but consciousness is nevertheless pure and directed towards an objective in this state. *The erring ego is, however, separated from the mechanism of implementation and, even in substitutions, is, with few exceptions, only separated from*

---

[9] Küppers, "Grundplan des Nervensystems u. Lokalisation des Psychischen," *Zsch. f. d. ges. Neur. u. Psychiat.*, 75 (1922), "Über den Ursprung und über die Bahnen der Willensimpulse," Ibid., 83 (1923), "Die psychol. Einheitlichkeit der Schizophrenie," *Zentbl. f. d. ges. Neur. u. Psychiat.*, 36, (1929) and *Schweiz. Arch. f. Neur. u. Psychiat.*, 26 (1930), "Über den Begriff der Grundstörung u. Ihre Bedeutung f. die Einteilung u. Lokaldiagnose der Geisteskrankheit," *Arch. f. Psychiat. u. Nervenkr.*, 99 (1933), "Der Weg zur Lokaldiagnose der Geisteskrankheiten," *Klin. Wochenschr.* 1933.

[10] *Arch. f. Psychiat. u. Nervenkr.*, 101 (1933) 69.

[11] Leroy, *Les visions du demisomeil*, Paris, Alcan, 1926.

[12] Gruhle, "Psychologie der Schizophrenie," *Zentbl. f. d. ges. Neur. u. Psychiat.*, 48 (1927).

part of the implementation. Only in a few cases does the subject temporarily forget his objective, and this loss of time is, if it occurs, merely a secondary consequence. For example, the objective is not lost if I dip my quill in my tea instead of in the ink.

A loss of goal, as a result of an incorrect implementation mechanism, occurs, by contrast, if I want to determine the room temperature from a thermometer on wall A, but, misled by a memory of the previous location of this instrument, walk to wall B and stare at a picture of Christ, above which the thermometer was hung for years, and, in the process, forget what I wanted. If I lose the objective of implementing an action at a certain stage, the implementation at this stage is carried out at a lower level of organization of the nervous system which works automatically in accordance with certain mechanical (biological and mechanical) principles which we will return to below. In other words, ego disorders in action substitutions as well as in other everyday errors do not represent complete passivity, as is the case in the hypnagogic state, but only passivity at a stage of implementation and this only temporarily, with the final objective always being kept in mind, except in a few cases.

Ego disorders of everyday errors reveal neither the consciousness disorder of dreams nor the dysfunction of schizophrenia. With respect to hypnagogic hallucinations, Küppers talks about the loss of mastery over the apparatus and says that the ego is, as it were, transcortical, while the motoric cerebral cortex is only an implementation organ of the ego. If we apply Küpper's theory to action substitutions as well as to all everyday errors committed by healthy persons, we can say that the mistakes are made by that cortical organization which has split off from intention and now works without its direction, as it were. Intention may have its origins in the orbital region, a theory that is given weight by Kleist's observations about personality changes following lesions of this cerebral region.

We must now answer the question of which factors thwart the automatic-mechanical (mechanical in the biological sense) working of the implementation apparatus of the ego. We will subdivide these factors into two groups and look at them one after the other:

<blockquote>
1. Attractions
2. Mental sets
</blockquote>

1. The attraction factors:
   a. The Ranschburg phenomenon, i.e. similarity inhibition based on homogeneous attraction,
   b. the suppression of differences partly as an attendant phenomenon of homogeneous inhibition, partly based on "heterogeneous abstraction," i.e. distraction.

2. The mental set factors:
    a) Perseveration and anticipation,
    b) The affect.

The so-called common errors are perseverative errors, but they are also anticipatory errors, since the common actions were not only often repeated prior to the error but will also recur after the error. Suggestion errors belong to affect errors, since there is no suggestion without affect. "Post-completion" errors and habitual errors are perseverative errors, as are errors made on the basis of the links of the connected theme.

1. Substitutions based on attraction

If we now review the 742 substitutions in our collection from this perspective, we find that *the substituted elements* of the action are, even at first glance, *partially identical*, i.e. homogeneous in the vast majority of cases. In other cases, this partial identity can be ascertained upon closer examination. Furthermore, a not insignificant number of, strictly speaking, heterogeneous substitutions display *partially identical characteristics in the holistic view of the overall situation*, i.e. in the environment. Cases which possess homogeneous characteristics neither partially nor in the overall situation and which are thus completely heterogeneous, are rare. Before summing up the statistics of our substitutions and before entering into a thorough discussion, we will provide examples for all of these categories.

Examples of substitutions of homogeneous objects: J. reaches for the inkpot instead of the teacup next to it (no. 11, two receptacles containing liquids); puts on slippers instead of shoes (no. 94, two types of footwear); takes out the gray instead of the red notebook (no. 164, two notebooks); is pouring dirty instead of clean water on the barley (no. 156), black coffee instead of milk into the cup (no. 279, two liquids); opens the upper instead of the lower sideboard drawer (no. 322), and the toothpick box instead of the ink pen box (no. 342); sprinkles salt instead of sugar on the cake (nos. 365, 411, 414, two white powders in similar shakers); puts hot instead of lukewarm water into his mouth (no. 420); hangs up the old instead of the new coat in the wardrobe (no. 439); puts a newspaper instead of writing paper into the drawer (no. 452, newspaper = paper); reaches for the water glass instead of the salt shaker (nos. 506, 515, two receptacles made of glass); takes a collection of poems instead of a dictionary to the porch (no. 626, two books); affixes a 40-cent stamp instead of a 20-cent stamp to a domestic letter (no 631); dips the pencil instead of the pen into the ink (no. 696, two writing utensils); dips the penholder instead of the pen (no. 714), on a different occasion a pencil into the ink (no. 771); reaches for manuscript A instead of manuscript B (no. 804); folds together the wrong instead of the right corners of a blanket (no. 865); is about to put the case instead of the glasses on his nose (no. 861); puts on a dirty instead of a clean shirt (no. 949); reaches for the shaving soap instead of the toilet soap (no. 951); and for the sponge instead of the soap (no. 1009, two washing items); picks up a handkerchief lying in front of his left hand instead of the blotting paper to dry the ink before turning the page (no. 1024, two thin white objects in the form of writing paper); reaches for the yellow quilt instead of the yellow pillow (no. 1031, two objects of the same color which belong on the bed).

A. pushes to me her teacup instead of mine (nos. 61, 62); puts on the black instead of the white apron (no. 84); is about to throw the hard-boiled egg instead of the egg shell into the fire (no. 109); puts the wrong instead of the right milk pot on the stove (no. 145); takes the wrong instead of the right tea (no. 247); puts the soap dish instead of the washbowl in the latter's position when rearranging the washstand (no. 271, two objects as washing utensils); puts on low shoes instead of ankle boots (no. 304); puts on the dirty instead of the clean apron (no. 340); puts the wrong instead of the right quilt on the bed (nos. 438, 458); reaches for the blue neck ribbon instead of the brown hair ribbon (no. 497); pours gasoline instead of spirit (no. 553), on another occasion water (no. 576) into the spirit burner (three liquids which are stored in bottles); starts to polish shoes with silver paste instead of shoe polish (no. 555); sprinkles salt instead of sugar on the cake (no. 589); gets out the lemon grater instead of the pumpkin cutter (no. 261); reaches for the chopper instead of the knife for cutting bread (no. 634); sprinkles flour instead of salt on the soup (no. 721); threads a blue instead of a white thread (no. 725); tries to open the writing desk drawer (no. 840) and, on another occasion, the bookcase with the wardrobe key (nos. 845, 846); is about to clean a silver spoon with toothpaste instead of silver polish (no. 866); pours spirit instead of vinegar on the beans (no. 981); lifts up one instead of another pot (no. 1015); reaches for the yellow blouse instead of the yellow scarf (no. 1085).

Examples of substitutions of partially identical places: J is about to put his glasses into his wallet instead of the glasses case (no. 1), the thermometer into the glasses case instead of its box (no. 45); carries the waste paper for lighting a fire (no. 6), on another occasion crockery (no. 91) into the bedroom instead of the kitchen; looks for his gloves in the wardrobe instead of on the writing desk (no. 101, two pieces of furniture in the same room); is about to pour dirty water into the garbage can instead of the dirty water tub (no. 116); puts the chocolate powder tin on the lower instead of the upper shelf board (no. 162); hangs a kitchen towel on a nail on the opposite wall instead of in its proper place (no. 206); looks for a handkerchief on the writing desk instead of in the wardrobe (no. 224); is about to spit the mouthwash water into the chamber pot instead of the dirty water tub (no. 338); puts a nasal probe in the right instead of the left washstand drawer (no. 359); puts the key to the writing desk drawer in the upper instead of the lower drawer lock (no. 435); when cleaning beans, throws the pods into the dish containing the cleaned beans instead of the dish for waste (no. 469); puts his glasses in the table drawer instead of on the table (no. 521); looks for the newspaper in room A instead of room B (no. 558); is about to put a book into the side section of the bookcase instead of the middle section (no. 605); bends down to spit into the teacup instead of the spittoon (no. 615, two bowls containing liquids); puts the washstand jug on the dirty water tub instead of in the wash basin (no. 703); is about to put the bread into the needlework basket instead of the bread basket (no. 706); looks for the paper scissors in the writing desk drawer instead of on the writing desk (no. 844); buttons the coat button into the buttonhole of his jacket instead of the coat (no. 805); tries to pull the pocket watch out of the right instead of the left vest pocket (no. 902); searches for the quilt case on a table far from the bedside table where it is usually placed (nos. 927, 928, 929); takes the spirit bottle to the table instead of to the crate where it belongs (no. 1003, crate and table are two pieces of kitchen furniture on which various kitchen utensils are placed); places it on the stove on another occasion (no 1033); searches for the writing paper in a book case section where it was stored in the past instead of the writing desk drawer (no. 1066).

In the evening A lies down on the chaise lounge instead of the bed (no. 71, two places to lie down in the bedroom); pours the tea into the coffee cup instead of the teacup (no. 103); pours the egg white into the egg yolk cup instead of the egg white cup (no. 127); adds butter to the compote instead of the vegetables (no. 176); pours spirit into the kitchenware instead of the spirit burner (no. 208); pours dirty water into the manure tub instead of the dirty water tub (no. 262); sews a button in the wrong place (no. 307); throws a burning piece of paper into the ash compartment of the stove instead of the fire (no. 336); takes water into her room instead of my room (no. 412); takes salt into the pantry instead of the room (no. 496); puts tea leaves into the greasy dish instead of the prepared tea dish (no. 550); puts milk on the spirit stove, which is not burning, instead of the stove (no. 585, two pieces of cooking equipment); carries the boiled milk into the room instead of the pantry (no. 651); drives a nail into the pantry wall instead of the kitchen wall (no. 668); carries a chair into the pantry instead of the anteroom (no. 738); sieves the tea onto a plate instead of into a cup (no. 783); is about to pour ground coffee into the milk instead of the water (no. 814); pours cornmeal into a measuring jug instead of a dish (no. 819); squeezes lemon juice into coffee instead of water (no. 922); puts her bed linen on my bed instead of her bed (no. 923); still half asleep in the morning, pours bismuth powder which she should take with water into the chamber pot instead of the water jar (no. 1023); searches for pastels in the drawer with oil colors instead of the drawer for pastels (no. 1094).

Examples of homogeneous movements. A. stands on a board instead of sitting on it (no. 100); she throws a duster out of the window instead of shaking it out (no. 719); fasten window bolts, locks and bars instead of opening them, or open them instead of fastening them in 32 cases; try to open doors to the inside, which open to the outside in 17 cases. J. arranges or browses through a manuscript nine times in reverse order, pull a necktie the wrong way through the collar (no. 68); A. knits plain instead of purl (no. 286). Most homogeneous substitutions of movements belong to the partial identity of the opposite.

Special consideration should be given to a few substitutions which, at first glance, seem to be heterogeneous but upon more thorough consideration turn out to be homogeneous. These include those instances where one of two objects is held in the left and the other in the right hand and are mistaken for one another during an action. In these cases it is not the two objects but the two hands which are the objects mistaken for one another. According to this perspective, these cases can thus be classified as homogeneous substitutions of objects.

Examples of the homogeneous substitution of the two hands holding things—J. wants (no. 4) to throw the nightcap, which he has in his right hand, onto the bed but raises his left instead of my right hand, which is nearer to the bed and in which he has the pocket watch he has just pulled out of his pocket; he is about to throw it onto the bed when he recognizes his mistake in time. The nightcap and the pocket watch are not partially identical, and thus there is no reason why they can be mistaken for one another because of being homogeneous. Both hands are, however, partially identical. Attraction works on the hand which is nearer to the bed. J. is about to throw (no. 844) his glasses instead of waste paper into the wastebasket. The glasses and the waste paper are not partially identical objects. But a closer look at this case reveals that J. had the waste paper in his left and the glasses in his right hand. In this case, too, both hands are partially identical; the right hand is nearer to the wastebasket and enjoys preference as the hand which is more often used and which is more willing to intervene during actions.

The same interpretation is true for case no. 1057 where the right hand is raised to throw the comb into the basket, the comb being accidentally held in this hand instead of the waste paper which is held in the left hand. For the same reason, the gloves held in the right hand in case 1081 are hung on the nail instead of the sleeping bag, which is held in the left hand, both hands being equidistant from the nail. In case 718 a glove held in the right hand is laid into the drawer instead of the lock held in the left hand, with both hands being an equal distance from the drawer. In case 1974 A., to help dry J.'s hands, gives me a newspaper, held by chance in her right hand, instead of the towel held in her left hand, with both of her hands being equally far away from J.

The many cases of right-left substitutions demonstrate that both hands are indeed the objects which have been mistaken for one another and not the objects held in the hands. Priority is given firstly to the hand which is nearer to the place where the objects should be put, and secondly to the right hand, which is more often used, more skilled, active and innervated. The fact that the two factors which determine the type of substitution (the primacy of the right hand and the proximity of the place around which action centers) compete with one another was demonstrated by one of the examples above.

The partial identity of the substituted objects can vary in degree and *imperceptibly change into heterogeneity.*

Examples of substitutions of objects with a lesser degree of partial identity. Substitutions of objects: J. intends (nos. 210, 632) to read the room temperature of the thermometer which is lying on the writing desk and instead looks at the pocket watch, which is lying next to the thermometer. The watch and the room thermometer are identical neither in form nor in color, but both have a scale, the watch a circular one and the thermometer a linear one, which is to be read. Both instruments answer homogeneous questions: "What time is it?" and "What temperature is it?" Partial identity thus also concerns the function of the objects mistaken for one another. The repetition of these types of mistakes – J. often made such mistakes before starting with his notes and after having terminated them -- also shows that it is correct to classify these cases as homogeneous substitutions. -- On another occasion (no. 236) J. looks at the thermometer instead of the watch. -- He accidentally holds a small round lock in the palm of his left hand in the way a pocket watch is held when the time should be read. At the same time, he is asked what time it is, whereupon he immediately raise the lock to his eyes to look at it. In this case, the reason for the partial identity is that the objects mistaken for one another have the same form, size and weight and that the small lock in the palm of the hand is held in the same way as a watch from which the time is read. The visual difference does not play a role, since J. raises the lock without looking at it. J. takes the materials and heads for the veranda to do some writing. He notices that he have forgotten to bring the scissors that he uses to separate the various notes taken down on the same piece of paper in order to arrange them according to objective criteria. He returns to the room, notices the ruler on his desk which he does not need at the moment but which he otherwise uses for making tables and takes it with him instead of the scissors. Despite all their differences, the scissors and the ruler are partially identical as writing utensils in this case.

Substitutions of place: A. cleans her shoes (no. 542) and puts the brush with a shoe instead of into the open drawer. In this case the shoe and the drawer provide two suggestively tempting openings which, at the same time, are accidentally close to one another when the brush is to be put away. A. is working in the kitchen, carries the flour to the stove and opens its door to throw the flour into the fire instead of carrying the flour into the pantry (no. 218). In this case, the partial identity of the two places is determined by the door of the stove and the door of the pantry.

The combined substitutions are usually not partially identical in all of their elements. We will come back to these cases.

Examples of combined substitutions with all elements being partially identical, substitution of objects + substitution of places: J. takes the pot with coffee from the lower shelf instead of taking the dish with milk from the floor (no. 302). The two receptacles containing liquids and mistaken for one another are partially identical. The pantry floor and the shelf, as storing places of food, can be regarded as partially identical. In the morning J. puts the nightcap on the bed instead of putting the cap in the wardrobe (no. 566). The nightcap and the cap are partially identical head gear. As pieces of furniture in the same room, which serve as storing places for both head gear, the bed and the wardrobe are partially identical.

Up to now, we have reviewed our substitutions for homogeneity in a so-to-speak "atomising" way, i.e. categorized the cases as to whether the grasped or intended objects, places, movements with the proper object at the proper place are wrong. The overwhelming majority of the substitutions specified demonstrate *the justification of this elementary analysis,* since the basis of homogeneity could be seen in this atomization from the first moment on. But in another series of our observations, this atomizing point of view turns out to be *inadequate* and prompts us to consider not only the individual elements of the substitutions but also their complex whole, and the more so since the elements cannot exist without this complex whole.

Even in the simplest case, when grasping an object, the grasping hand, the object, the place where the object is, to which and from which it is taken, and also the movement and the acting person are united in an integral whole. We have said that the action, when it is translated into language, is corresponding to a theorem of action. In the totality of the theorem of action, that which turns out to be useful is called the unity of the theorem[13] in the psychology of language; when it is translated into our terms, it can be expressed as the unity of the *unity of the theorem of action.*

The aspect of totality allows us to discern *homogeneous characteristics in the totality* of the environment of the individual factors, even in elements which are heterogeneous as far as the object, the place or the movement is concerned, and to recognize that it is this homogeneity which has started

---

[13] S. Bruno Sondeck, Der Satz als Einheit und die Satzarten. Arch. f. d. ges. Psychol. **94** (1935).

the substitution.

This category of substitutions includes those cases where heterogeneous objects are mistaken for one another because of their homogeneous location. Here the place and the object form an integral whole such that the object and the place cannot be separated from one another. The present location in the same place constitutes the one category of these cases, whereas in the other cases potential storing places of the objects are concerned.

Examples of heterogeneous object substitutions based on the homogeneity of their present location: J. intends to take a package containing quinine powder from the writing desk and put it into the medicine cupboard, but instead he takes the pocket watch, which is also lying on the writing desk, into his hands, carries it to the medicine cupboard and only then discovers his mistake (no. 22). The quinine powder package and the pocket watch are dissimilar objects. That the two objects are side-by-side on the writing desk makes it necessary to regard the watch and its present location as a whole, in which the package and the writing desk are included. But on the other hand, the pocket watch is also connected with the writing desk because of its present location.

If the objects mistaken for one another are heterogeneous, their location on the writing desk is a homogeneous characteristic of two homogeneous objects: 1. the package with quinine powder and 2. the pocket watch on the desk. No attempt is made to use this opinion to introduce homogeneity in an artificial way (where it does not exist) only to constrain it within the framework of a well-known law. It is clear that the quinine package could not have been mistaken for the watch had not both been lying on the desk side by side.

If, for example, another object, e.g. a small purse, instead of the watch had been lying on the desk, the quinine powder package and the small purse could have been mistaken for one another as well, because their joint location on the desk would have been a common homogeneous characteristic of their integral whole. If, on the other hand, the quinine powder package and the pocket watch had not been lying on the desk side by side, and, thus, their joint location were not a common characteristic, (if, for example, the quinine powder package had been left in the wardrobe erroneously) the package in the wardrobe would in all probability not have been mistaken for the pocket watch on the desk. Rather, it would have been mistaken for an object in the wardrobe, if there had been a substitution, since the location in the wardrobe would have been the homogeneous characteristic of both totalities.

If we were to continue atomization, we could perhaps say that in the case discussed above, not the objects but the grasps for them at two adjacent places on the desk that had been mistaken for one another. Then it ought to be added here that all this does not only include the wrong grasp at two places on the desk but also the wrong process of grasping and the carrying away of a heterogeneous object. It can be seen that this atomizing way of looking at things is inadequate and leads us to the totality view. -- From the verandah J. Goes into the room where he wants to read. Upon entering the room, he automatically tends to take off his hat, but instead of that, reaches for his glasses which are on my nose and takes them off. The hat and the glasses are heterogeneous objects. But if one, on the one hand, regards the glasses and their present location on the nose and before the eyes and the side pieces around the ears as a totality and, on the other, the hat and its present location on the head as another totality, we have two partially identical totalities:

1. the glasses on the head, 2. the hat on the head. Also in this case it can be said that this is a substitution of two homogeneous reaches for two adjacent points on the head, but then a second heterogeneous substitution ought to be assumed, and we finally arrive at the same conclusion as in the former case. What is also certain in this case is that the glasses and the hat had not been mistaken for one another because they are heterogeneous objects but because of the homogeneous characteristic of their being a totality which is based on their homogeneous location (no. 47). This substitution also implies an anticipation which means that thinking is directed towards the glasses which are necessary for reading, and, since the glasses are where they belong, a misleading inducement takes place which we are going to illustrate by giving further misleading substitutions. -- In the substitutions where J. grasps the box instead of the knife (nos. 2 and 29), these heterogeneous objects are also lying side by side on the work top of the kitchen buffet. The same holistic principle on the basis of the location of the erroneously grasped object can be applied to the substitutions where the gloves were grasped instead of the newspaper (no. 131), the coffee cup was grasped instead of the matchbox (no. 165), the water jar instead of the glasses (no. 168), the watch instead of the glasses (no. 447), on another occasion the cap (no. 735), a notebook instead of the body thermometer (no. 204) which were accidentally lying in the same location.--The following are somewhat different substitutions which are, however, understandable because of the existing totality: J wants to take the spirit burner from the pantry but instead of that takes a small dish with fat, because the latter is standing on the spirit burner accidentally and is therefore readily within reach.--A. takes out a board instead of a washcloth (No, 398). The two objects are principally heterogeneous, but in this case they belong to a whole, since this board is otherwise put on a washstand, a wash basin onto the washstand and the washcloth into the wash basin. Thus, the washcloth and the board as washing utensils become partially identical as far as their function and location are concerned. The partial identity is also

demonstrated by the fact that the connection between the two objects gives rise to the substitution. -- A wants to throw bread to the dog, but instead of that throws the bread knife to him (no. 583). The bread and the knife, which are principally heterogeneous, become a totality because of their joint location in the bread basket to which the function of the knife, the cutting of bread, is added.

The totality view brings to bear homogeneous characteristics, even in those cases where two principally heterogeneous locations become partially identical as storing places of objects.

Examples of substitutions of principally heterogeneous locations which are of a secondary partial identity as storing places of objects: J. is looking for the key to the anteroom in the kitchen buffet drawer, instead of on the anteroom hook where it belongs. The hook and the drawer are heterogeneous, but, as component parts of a whole, they have one partially identical characteristic, since various household keys are hanging on this hook, but another key, including the lock, is usually lying in the kitchen buffet drawer (no. 215). -- The same way of thinking applies to case 297, where a coat pocket is searched for a key.

In case 1032, where J. wants to put the glasses which are lying on the writing desk into the case but searches for the glasses on his nose, two heterogeneous locations, the nose and the writing desk, are mistaken for one another, i.e. two locations where the glasses usually are and where they obtain a secondary partial identity. That here homogeneity is the determining factor of the substitution can be seen in the fact that the nose and the writing desk, the hook and the kitchen buffet drawer or the coat pocket could only be mistaken for one another because of the connection described, i.e. the secondary partial identity. Mental health taken for granted, this substitution could not happen without the connection described. No mentally healthy person will use the hammer to knock onto the coat pocket instead of the hook or hold his handkerchief in front of the writing desk instead of his nose. These would be examples of substitutions of the same locations but without the connection which gave rise to the substitution, since the locations would then have lost their secondary partial identity.

The *holistic view* is also of decisive importance in the combined substitutions which do not refer to one element of the action, i.e. only to the object, the location or the movement, but refer to several elements at the same time, that is to say in a way the substitution is heterogeneous in one or two of the elements and partially identical in one or two of the other elements. *Then the partially identical elements also extend the substitution to the heterogeneous elements.* The atomizing analysis does not suffice, since the heterogeneous elements are not mistaken for one another if the partially identical ones were not to play a leading role. To understand the phenomenon of the substitution of heterogeneous elements in these combined cases we have to bear in mind that these cases do not imply anything principally new.

This phenomenon was already included in the substitution of one element since in the latter cases the individual mistaken objects, locations and movements had never been identical but only partially identical, that is to say they had not only identical but also heterogeneous characteristics which had been disregarded because of the leading role of the identical characteristics. (We will come back to this "suppression of differences" which I described 20 years ago.) If, for example, a yellow blouse instead of a yellow scarf is reached for there are not only identical characteristics which are provided by the color, the fabric and the fact of being an article of clothing but also a number of differing characteristics as the shape, the buttons and buttonholes of the blouse, the way of putting it on etc.

In the combined action substitutions, the same phenomenon of the "suppression of differences" will only be extended since that which happens to the differing characteristics of one element will also apply to the other differing elements. In the same way as we regard the element of an action, if it is mistaken with another one, and the differing characteristics of this element, e.g. the scarf or the blouse, as a complex whole, as a totality, so do we have to consider the entire action including its heterogeneous and homogeneous elements as totalities when dealing with the combined substitutions. Even if this totality view is necessary, it would still be wrong to neglect the analysis of the characteristics and elements as though they were not existing at all.

Examples of combined substitutions with partially similar and partially dissimilar elements. Object +place substitutions: J. wants to know the room temperature and, for this purpose, goes to wall B instead of wall A and looks at the picture of Christ instead of the thermometer, without knowing this very moment what he wanted to do (no. 8). The picture of Christ and the thermometer are dissimilar elements of the action, but the two walls and the location of the objects, which are both hanging on walls, are partially identical. As a result of the wholes, 1. the picture of Christ on wall B and 2. the thermometer on wall A, there exists a partial identity of these wholes and thus a partial identity of the entire action, which, on the one hand, leads to the Ranschburg phenomenon, and, on the other, suppresses the heterogeneous characteristics of the two walls and the homogeneity of the elements: icon of Christ and thermometer.

Object + movement substitutions: A. wants to take the floor lamp out of the bedroom (no. 1050) and instead screws in the bulb from the bedroom hanging lamp which has been screwed out halfway. The two movements, the screwing out and screwing in are dissimilar. On the whole, however, the screwing out and the screwing in of the bulb means that the light is switched on. Furthermore, the floor and the hanging lamps are partially identical. J. wants to put the bedside lamp on the table (no. 879), but instead of that pulls the contact of the bedside lamp out of the hanging lamp. The purely atomistic analysis of the case produces the following result: Here, the mistaken objects which have been reached for are partially identical: the bedside lamp and the contact of the hanging lamp which switches on the current in the bedside lamp. The bedside table, on which the bedside lamp should be placed and the switching point of the hanging lamp from where the contact had been pulled out are heterogeneous locations. It is a matter of discussion whether the putting down of the lamp and the pulling out of the contact should be regarded as partially identical. The one existing partial identity: the bedside lamp and the contact suffices to result in the substitution of the entire action, including its heterogeneous elements.

According to the totality view, the statement can be made that two actions where two electrical lamps had been affected had been mistaken for one another. In cases 58 and 59 J. goes into A's bedroom to take a pot from there and bring it to his room. Upon entering A's room, he notices that the electrical lamp which is standing on the bedside table has not been switched on and is not standing in the place where it belongs. Instead of taking the pot out of the bedside table, J. switches on the floor lamp and leaves the room re bene gesta. Here, the object substitution is heterogeneous, since, instead of the pot, the bedside lamp has been reached for. According to the holistic view of the location, the two heterogeneous objects, the pot and the lamp, become partially identical since one of the objects has been standing in, the other one on the bedside table. The locations from where both objects are taken are partially identical, whereas the putting down of the lamp and the switching on of the contact can be rather thought of as differing movements. -- In case 63, this process is repeated, but the difference is that J., who enters A's room with the same purpose in mind, recognizes that the floor lamp is already where it belongs and mistakes this action carried out before for the action intended to be carried out in the present.

Also these cases confirm the need for viewing objects in connection with their location, which does not at all mean that the elementary analysis might be dispensed with. Quite the opposite is true, namely that the elementary analysis fully serves to illustrate the importance of the whole.

We have said that the partial identity of the mistaken elements manifests itself by degrees, which gradually change into complete heterogeneity. Apart from the fully similar substitutions, we came across these transitions in those cases where the heterogeneity of the objects and locations could only be identified upon careful consideration and in cases where the heterogeneous objects possessed similar characteristics as far as their total location was concerned. Up to now, it had not been necessary to consider that all these action substitutions did not only include elements which had been mistaken but also some which had not been mistaken. This was, for example, true for the case where two objects were lying on the table and the wrong heterogeneous or homogeneous one had been reached for, the substitutions on the table and the movements being almost fully identical.

We will now come across another transition to complete heterogeneity in those substitutions where not only the completely heterogeneous objects and the completely heterogeneous locations were mistaken, but the movements of action were correct, and they were identical for both cases. Our collection includes two of these cases which have to be analyzed in detail.

2. *Cases of dissimilar object and place substitutions*: J. asks A. to pass him the red notebook, which is lying close to her on the small table. In this very moment she catches sight of a thread torn off the mat-like carpet lying in front of her, picks it up immediately, because of her sense of order, and passes it to him. The thread and the notebook are completely heterogeneous, and also the floor and the table, although they are connected due to their location. That part of the action which has not been mistaken for another element of the action, namely the movement of passing, is identical (no. 871). -- J. reaches for the tissue in his coat pocket instead of the cap which is lying on the table. Not only the paper and the cap, but also the table and the coat pocket, are completely heterogeneous. The movements of reaching for the object and grasping it, which have not been mistaken, are identical. The substitution is an anticipation of a process which makes it necessary to reach for the cap, whereas it is unnecessary to reach for the paper since it is always handy in the pocket (no. 199).

These two substitutions include important factors which we did not come across until now. In our previously analyzed cases it was the homogeneous characteristics of the objects, places and movements, or the homogeneous characteristics of the total situation, which gave rise to the substitution. But in these two cases the substitution had not been governed by homogeneous attraction. Catching sight of the heterogeneous thread on the floor *did not* constitute a homogeneous attraction but an *abstraction* from the action. Therefore, the choice of the wrong object and location had been determined by abstraction, but we can also call it *distraction*. The ego had been split off from the task for this part of the action but then returned to it when the person already had the wrong object in his or her hands. Only then the location of the wrong object in the hand and the object constituted a totality. The location of the notebook in the hand would have been the other totality. In the totality of the situation, this location itself included the homogeneous element which gave rise to the substitution. In the second case, the abstractive element entered the action by anticipation.

Since this abstractive element became effective and resulted in the heterogeneous object being grasped at a dissimilar location, the connection between both elements which were necessary for the action and their environment also manifested itself. Thus, we have to count these doubly, e.g. in the object and in the location heterogeneous substitutions among those which will be explained by the view of totality.

After having dealt with these gradual transitions we will now discuss those *rare cases where objects, places and movements were mistaken for one another.* Since these are related to previous cases in which only one or two elements had been confused, we can count them among the substitutions. The fact that an action has been replaced by another one also speaks in favor of this view, although common usage refuses to accept the term "substitution" in the sense of "confusion" and would rather tend to accept "substitution" in the sense of "replacement". There are three cases of this kind which must be discussed in more detail.

3.Cases of object, place and movement substitutions which are dissimilar in all elements: J. goes from the verandah, where he was doing a writing job, into his room to take a sheet of ruled paper out of the writing desk drawer. But he caught sight of a wasp on the window pane of the room, kills it with a flyswatter and returns to the verandah, as if he had done his job properly. The wasp, the sheet of ruled paper, the killing and the process of taking out something, the window pane and the writing desk drawer are completely heterogeneous (no. 627).

J takes a jug with hot water to his room and wants to empty the water into the wash basin on the washstand to wash his hands. Because it is too dark in the room at night, he put the jug on the washstand without emptying it and without washing his hands. He then puts on the light by turning the switch and goes away. From an atomizing viewpoint this would mean that two heterogeneous graspable objects are mistaken for one another: the hot water jug for the light switch. Then there are two heterogeneous locations: the wall for the switch and the washstand for the jug. And finally there are two heterogeneously pure actions, the turning of the switch and the emptying of the jug, to be followed by the washing of the hands. According to the holistic view, the emptying of the hot water jug and the washing of hands are being confused with the lighting of the room (no. 908).

J. intends to put a torn-off button on the washstand in A's room, where he usually puts such things. J. has the button in his hands and goes to A's room where he catches sight of the window and remembers that he should open the window for airing the room. He opens the window with the button in his hand and leaves the room with the button still in his hand. From an atomizing point of view, this would mean that the heterogeneous objects: the button and the window latch; the heterogeneous locations: the window and the washstand; the heterogeneous movements: the putting down of the button and the opening of the latch and of the window are mistaken for one another. According to the holistic view, the statement is that J. had opened the window instead of putting down the button (no. 472).

Without any doubt, the reader will have noticed that these completely heterogeneous substitutions will differ in many respects from the homogeneous, or those heterogeneous ones which possess heterogeneous characteristics in the totality of the environment, since the intended action in those substitutions which are heterogeneous in all of their elements is replaced by a completely different one. What can be added is that the intended action has been forgotten by distraction; but a substitution, e.g. when the blotting paper is mistaken for the handkerchief, cannot be explained by forgetfulness. Owing to this, many a reader will tend to count the cases among the omissions. And we would have as much right to assume an omission of the blotting paper and the inkpot when the handkerchief is mistaken for the blotting paper or the teacup for the inkpot or an omission of the outside movement of the door when the door is erroneously tried to be opened to the outside instead of the inside.

If we were to regard all of these cases as <u>*omissions*</u> *we would also have to use the term* <u>*insertion*</u> *to cover the entire phenomenon,* since we cannot say that the forgotten action had been omitted in the completely heterogeneous cases, and the blotting paper or the inkpot in the other cases, without having to add that the completely heterogeneous action, and otherwise the teacup or the handkerchief, had been inserted. According to this elementary analysis any substitution = insertion + omission. So considering a substitution does already imply a view of totality as opposed to the elementary analysis. After all, these thoughts show that substitutions, omissions and insertions are not categories but manifestations of the errors, which should not mean that these manifestations should not be separately analyzed and, therefore, differentiated from one another.

In the following we compile the statistics on homogeneous and heterogeneous substitutions:

Out of 742 substitutions:
675 are similar
64 are dissimilarity-based with similar totality characteristics
3 are completely dissimilar

According to Ranschburg, the phenomenon described by him is based on the homogeneous attraction which has not been attributed the same importance in literature as the homogeneous inhibition, since it was only considered to be the theoretical foundation of the homogeneous inhibition.

This homogeneous attraction also escaped my notice when I dealt with it as an up-to-then unknown phenomenon in my work on reading errors. It almost looks as if the homogeneous inhibition had a homogeneously inhibitory effect as a result of its partial identity with the homogeneous attraction which had, after all, come to my knowledge, and as if this had also been true for other researchers.

In my work on reading errors I dealt with such omissions where the eyes involuntarily miss out a line and, therefore, one or two lines of text are omitted. In the text passages where the eyes started wandering, partially identical or identical words were considered to be triggering mechanisms for missing out one or two lines of text. It was really impressive to experience directly a homogeneous attraction and see how a homogeneous reading text appearing as a marginal object in the field of vision attracts the eyes in such a way that they are centered on this homogeneous reading text.

In his early works Ranschburg described this homogeneous attraction as the cornerstone of his doctrine, and since then he has returned to this problem in several works[14] and presented this homogeneous attraction as a much more general physiological, chemical and physical law. In his book "Az emberi elme", he also refers to the Hungarian poet Imre (Emerich) Madách[15], who, in his dramatic poem, described the attraction of related persons and objects as a law. But Madách also refers to *the repulsion of the opposite,* which is in line with my *suppression of differences*, which will be dealt with later on.

My present collection of action substitutions includes a significant number of cases where *the homogeneous attraction was also present in the mental experience*, which should not mean, however, that it is only effective in these cases. On the contrary, it has to be acknowledged that it must be included in each homogeneous inhibition, since it is the underlying principle, but awareness of this homogeneous attraction is not the same for every case. In the action substitutions of my collection, different kinds of homogeneous attractions have been experienced; in the first case the eyes were attracted by the wrong homogeneous objects and places and the respective movements directed towards the homogeneous object or place. In the second case, a wrong object almost automatically fell into the searching hands, and, in the third case, the object, place or movement barred the preceding line of thought.

Examples of substitutions where the similarity attraction was included in the

---

[14] Ranschburg, J. f. Psychol. u. Neur. 1905 - Zsch. f. Psychol. 66-67 (1913)- - Dtsch. Zsch. f. Nervenhk. 1913. - Zentbl. f. d. ges. Neur. u. Psychiat. 1926 - Arch. ital. psicol. 11 (1933) - Neederlandsch Tydschr. f. Psychol. 1934 - Das krankhafte Gedächtnis. Leipzig, Barth, 1911. - Az emberi elme (ungarisch) Budapest 1023 - Die Lese- und Schreibstörungen des Kindesalters. Halle a. S., Marhold, 1928.

[15] In his "Tragödie des Menschen" written in 1859, in the scene set in the future, MADÁCH reports the scholar and Lucifer to have said:

experience of the action substitution: J. puts on a slipper instead of a shoe, because his eyes were attracted by it (no. 94); looked for the toothbrush in another washstand dish instead of the dish where it is usually kept, after catching sight of the dish where the toothbrush was previously kept (no. 86); is about to spit the mouthwash which he took into his mouth from the glass held in his right hand into the empty glass held in his left hand instead of the wash tub, because this glass is near to his eyes and also to his mouth (no. 110); instead of the respective notebook he is about to enter a note into a sheet of his manuscript, because his hand is resting on it (attraction of grasp no. 191); instead of the respective hook he hangs a kitchen towel on a hook on the opposite wall, because he caught sight of this hook (no. 206); he waits for a visitor who is coming by bus but catches sight of the people arriving with the incoming nearby local train, looks them over, because his eyes are attracted by the people, although he knows that the expected guest is not arriving by train (no. 347); turns on the wrong instead of the right electrical switch, since the wrong switch is closer and within easy reach (no. 554); takes a dictionary instead of a volume of poems in his hands, because he caught sight of the dictionary (no. 626); put on a wrong instead of the right pair of gloves for the same reason (no. 731); put a wrong instead of the right lid on the cooking pot (no. 802); put the dirty instead of a clean shirt on (no. 949), since in all these cases the glance skimmed over the wrong object and did not release the object; tried to dry his writing with a handkerchief instead of the blotting paper, because his left hand was resting on it while holding the pen in his right hand (no. 1024).

A. is going to rub the slipper instead of the shoe with shoe polish, because her left hand happened to be near the slipper (no. 80, attraction of grasp); pours the gravy into the dirty water tub instead of the respective dish (no. 136), and the spirit into a cooking pot instead of the spirit burner, since her glance fell on these two objects; grasps a larger instead of a smaller needle because the latter is falling into her searching hands (no. 317); pours the cocoa powder into the curd cheese cup instead of the milk cup because she is anticipating a manipulation involving the curd cheese (thinking attraction no. 440); is about to polish the shoe with the silver polish instead of the shoe polish because the polish is lying directly in front of her eyes (no. 555); lights the fire in the stove instead of the spirit burner, since the stove is more appealing (no. 649); pours the tea into the plate which she is seeing in front of herself instead of the cup (no. 783); reaches for the wardrobe key instead of the writing desk key, because the former is almost falling into her hands (no. 840); instead of the hand lamp she reaches for the bulb of the hanging lamp because her first glance is on the latter (no. 1050).

In the similar grasping process, the right hand where the object is sometimes held as a result of an earlier activity is generally the preferred one. If wrongly grasped objects are lying closer than those which should have been grasped, they are usually lying closer to the right hand. If two objects have been confused with one another, one of which was held in the right and the other one in the left hand, right-handers will be doing this with their right hand in the majority of cases. It would be interesting to note whether this right-handedness in the process of grasping would be accompanied by a "right-eye tendency"[16] in the process of looking. Unfortunately, I did not take this aspect under consideration. When the location was recorded in my reports the wrong object attracting the eyes was lying directly in front of the person.

We are now turning to the other important phenomenon of the substitutions: to the suppression of heterogeneity, which is of utmost importance in addition to and independently of the homogeneity inhibition. It will never be the case that the objects mistaken for one another are completely identical, and if they are not completely identical, this does in itself mean that the assimilation of the two mistaken objects, locations or movements has the effect to fuse the identical elements but also to suppress or at least not take into consideration differing characteristics. In this one form of suppressing differences the point is that the homogeneous inhibition caused by the homogeneity attraction will lead to the attendant phenomenon of the suppression of differences.

Examples of the suppression of heterogeneity as an aftereffect of the homogeneity inhibition. If J. puts the glass where the caraway is stored on a lower shelf of the rack instead of the proper one, the identical characteristics of the shelves amalgamate as mental images and thus cause the confusion while the differing characteristics of the two shelves, their different height and also the visual image of all objects standing there, are being ignored (no. 1007). If J. reaches for the sponge instead of the soap, it is because they have identical characteristics when being used as washing utensils; these amalgamate as mental images and initiate the substitution whereas the numerous differing characteristics , the differing forms and colors are not taken into consideration but are suppressed (no. 1009). In the same way we can examine all our homogeneous substitutions and, apart from the identical characteristics the mental images of which have amalgamated, specify the heterogeneous characteristics which have been ignored.

In my work dating from 1918, I made a distinction between amalgamation and assimilation and understood the reading of the series of the letters a b b c as a b c, that is to say the reading of the two b's as one b

---

[16] In his "Tragödie des Menschen" written in 1859, in the scene set in the future, MADÁCH reports the scholar and Lucifer to have said:

as the first stage and the simplest form of the process, as a mere amalgamation, because two identical elements were fused. I regard the reading of m or n instead of mn as the second stage. In the second stage, an assimilation process takes place, since an excess stroke of m is assimilated. But this excess stroke is still identical with the two other strokes of m and the stroke of n. This excess stroke is the characteristic which distinguishes m from n, in itself it is not a differing characteristic as for example the stroke which (among other things) distinguishes t from l. The third stage is the suppression of the differing characteristic, e.g. the stroke in t, if l is written instead of t. In this suppression of differences the differences are completely assimilated. It is this suppression of differences which is an indispensable element of each action substitution. If we thus want to continue to use Wundt's expression 'assimilation is to be distinguished from amalgamation'.

It was most important for us to note in which cases the grasped objects are in themselves heterogeneous and partially identical characteristics can be found among the characteristics of the complex whole, i.e. in this case the location of the objects in their environment. In these cases the location, i.e. the partially identical characteristics of the complex whole, bring about the substitution. Also in these cases the homogeneous attraction is the triggering mechanism of the substitution. The number of the heterogeneous characteristics is here much greater than in the substitution of the similar objects, since, in the first place, the confused objects are completely differing, and, in the second, their side-by-side location on the same table, because they are, for example, not in the same place on the table, is also partially identical, that is to say, also only partially differing. In those cases where locations which are heterogeneous in themselves are partially identical as storing places of objects, that is to say, as storing places, the number of the differing characteristics is also large. But since, for example, a nail and a coat pocket or a nail and a sideboard drawer were mistaken for one another because of their common characteristic as a storing place, here amalgamation was also brought about by the homogeneous attraction and inhibition and resulted in the suppression of differences.

The suppression of the differing elements as an aftereffect of the homogenous attraction and inhibition is also quite obvious in those combined substitutions whose elements were partially homogeneous and partially heterogeneous. In most of these cases the homogeneous attraction and inhibition seem to be of primary and the suppression of differences of secondary importance. But in a minority of these cases distraction is also of concern as in the substitutions nos. 58, 59 and 63 where J., going into A's bedroom, instead of taking the pot from the bedside, switched on the lamp which was standing on the bedside table. Here the heterogeneity of the bedside table might have caused the substitution, since J. walked to the bedside table. The following erroneous stage of the action must be subjected to a different interpretation than the remaining substitutions where the differences of the objects were ignored, for in this very case the object which is heterogeneous in itself underwent abstraction. The point is not that the heterogeneity bent over our work. There is a window opposite to us. Suddenly the figure of a man walking along the street appears in the upper periphery of our fields of vision. We raise our heads as if in a sudden reflex and focus our eyes on the figure. We realize that it is a foreigner walking by and then we continue our work. In this case, the error was only a short break in our work, whereas, in another case, the same event may distract a person from trains of thought or a conversation. In a biological sense this distraction and its concomitant suppression of differences often constitutes a protection mechanism aimed at warding off a danger, and it must therefore work like a quick reflex since any reflection on a proper response would take too long. Even if there is no imminent danger from outside for anyone sitting inside, the biological protection mechanism is not able to adjust to these differences because of the required speed of the response. Any subsequent differentiated reasoning will be adequate. (In certain cases, such reasoning will be completely absent. So for example, monkeys in a cage attack one another upon hearing a sudden noise, e.g. a nearby shot, without realizing what has happened.)

At the beginning of this study we stated that the intention of the acting person is split away from the execution of the task in errors of action, either during one stage or in the whole of the action. In the general use of the German language this splitting away is termed absent-mindedness. As far as a common type of absent-mindedness is concerned, it usually entails unfamiliar trains of thought which have a distracting effect; in the Romance languages the words "distrait, distratto" are used for this. The distraction may, however, only affect the mechanism, the ultimate goal being kept in mind. In those cases also, where the trains of thought are of an unfamiliar nature, it is a suppression of differing mental images and processes. The Ranschburg inhibition may occur in healthy persons if they are distracted or if the time spent on reading a text did not suffice to take it in. In the first case distraction, and in the second the impossibility to take in the text, result in the production of an error; whereas it is established by the similar inhibition which objects, locations or movements are confused or omitted. The occurrence of either an omission or a substitution, on the other hand, seems to depend on the nature of intention. In addition to that, the mental setting factors, which we now turn to, also have a decisive effect.

2. The Mental Set

Perseveration, including its concomitant anticipation, can be regarded as belonging to the mental set. The so-called common errors fall under perseveration since they are habitual repetitions. But in the repetitive daily actions they also include an anticipatory component, since these actions will also repeat themselves in the future, and the resultant mental set regarding this future must be taken into consideration. Hermann Weimer[17] counts the anticipations among the perseverations; and Weimer and Mayer and Wundt as well have already stated that language encompasses an anticipatory element. This relationship is not only manifest in the actions but also in speaking and writing. The anticipatory element can be reflected in the experience created. If I really rank the perseverative errors among the concepts of the mental set, this view is in agreement with that of Hermann Weimer, which emphasizes the perseverative character of the mental set. If I furthermore use mental set as the generic term for perseveration the reason is that the mental set comprises a larger number of phenomena. As far as the affect errors are concerned, the affect is the factor that determines the mental set. An "enhancement controlled by one's will" (e.g. "an enormous quantity" instead of a "quantity"), which was investigated by Hermann Weimer, is also an affect error. If suggestion produces errors it must be emphasized that any suggestion is based on affect. The perseverative errors in the mental set also include those which I, going back to Herbart 20 years ago, counted as due to the law of the commenced melody[18] , which means that a series a b c d e, once started and ended, tends to run through to the end when started again and crush anything in its way with its dynamic force.

Since all of our 742 substitutions belong partly to the attractive and partly to the distractive errors, and since the mental set also plays an important part, using a Freudian expression we can say that these errors suffer from "multiple excessive determinations".

Examples of perseverative mental set errors. Object substitutions. J tries (82) to introduce a thick cotton-wool tampon into the left and then a thinner tampon into the narrower right nostril. After having introduced the thick left tampon he also prepares a thick instead of a thinner tampon for the right nostril; he looks (no. 236) at the thermometer instead of the cloc, after having read the thermometer before.

Place substitutions: J. searches (no. 34) for a clock in the lower instead of the upper drawer, because he had just taken an object out of this drawer.

Movement substitutions: A. tries (no's. 140, 158, 214, 239, 280) to open the

---

[17] Hermann Weimer. Psychologie der Fehler. Klinkhardt, Leipzig 1929. 2nd edition, p. 31 ff.

[18] For von Monakov and Mourque, actions include a kinetic melody.

verandah door, which opens to the outside, to the inside because the anteroom door, through which she went to the verandah, opens to the inside. The multiple repetition of the same error, a subsequent error according to Weimer's nomenclature, can also be attributed to perseveration.

Combined substitutions: In case no. 8, which has been discussed several times, where I look at the picture of Christ on wall B instead of the thermometer on wall A, perseveration exercises a certain influence, because the thermometer had been hanging at another place over the picture two years ago and was read several times. A. (no. 308) wants to pick up the dirt from the floor by using a shovel but instead of the shovel she takes a cloth, and, instead of picking up the dirt she smudges it on the floor, because she previously wiped the floor with a wet cloth.

Anticipating perseverations. Object substitution: (no's. 904, 914) J. reaches for the cotton wool instead of the fever thermometer, because he intends to use the oily cotton wool after having taken the rectal temperature and has already prepared it; J. reaches into the salt instead of the spoons, since he thought of the salt, which he wanted to take out of the dish with a spoon.

Place substitutions: J. (no. 1020) searches for the sponge in the washstand drawer instead of in the dish where it is usually kept, because his thinking was already focussed on the next step, that is to say, the taking of a comb out of this drawer; J. (no. 1084) was to put the coal shovel into the kitchen coal box after having made a fire in the stove, but instead of this he carries it to the kitchen washstand, because his thinking is focussed on the idea that he is going to wash his dirty hands .

There are two different kinds of substitutions among those in which the perseveration and anticipation are equally important elements. In the first kind of substitutions it is the frequency of the everyday actions which, as we have said, occurred as frequently in the past as they will occur in the future, and for the first reason they have a perseverative and for the second reason an anticipatory component. In the second kind of substitutions it is not the frequency of the past and future everyday activities that is concerned but the fact that certain directly preceding or directly following actions have a before-or-after effect.

Examples of perseveration and anticipation based on the frequency of occurrence: Object substitution. J. (nos. 750, 752, 753) has switched off the electrical light of the hanging lamp by turning the bulb, for reasons that are not of interest here. In order to switch on the light he should turn the bulb, but instead of that he reaches for the switch by the door upon entering the room. The light was switched on and will be switched on more frequently by turning the switch than by turning the bulb, which has to happen only once per day. In contrast to that, the reverse error, namely the attempt to turn the bulb instead of turning the switch does not appear in my records. J.

(no. 632) looks at his pocket watch instead of the thermometer, since the measurement of time is a more frequently repeated action than the measurement of the room temperature, both in the past and in the future.

Place substitutions: Coming out of the room J. Wants to put an object into the anteroom (no. 1096), but from the anteroom he turns to A's bedroom, since in the process of coming out of his room every day in the past and in the future, he more frequently turns to go to her bedroom than to the anteroom; A, coming out of J's room (no. 1092) carries an object to her room instead of the kitchen, since turning to her room happened more frequently in the past and is going to happen more frequently in the future.

Examples of perseveration and anticipation as a result of actions carried out directly before or directly after an action . Object substitutions. A. puts the soap dish instead of the wash basin on the floor (no. 917), because she had previously used the soap and intends to wash herself; Anna (no. 229) puts a cup instead of the piece of bread on a plate. *Perseveration*: Just a moment ago she put the cup on the table. *Anticipation*: The next action is pouring the tea into the cup.

Place substitutions: Someone in the kitchen asks J. (no. 6) to take waste paper out of his room and carry it into the kitchen. Although the voice can be heard from the kitchen, J. carries the waste into the bedroom. J. has just been to the bedroom and is preparing to go to bed; A. (no. 961) carries the coffee into her room instead of the kitchen table. She has just been to this room and is going to return there; For the same reason she (no. 683) carries the leftovers into her room instead of the pantry.

My statistics about perseveration and anticipation in the substitutions is as follows:

$$386 \text{ negative cases} = 52.00\,\%$$
$$156 \text{ perseverations} = 21.04\,\%$$
$$33 \text{ anticipations} = 22.51\,\%$$
$$67 \text{ perseverations and anticipations} = 4.45\,\%$$
$$\text{Total } 742 = 100\%$$

After we had been able to compile a statistics of 52 % negative and 48 % positive perseveration and anticipation errors the following deficiencies have to be taken into consideration in the assessment of these figures. Perseverations and anticipations should include not only those substitutions whose following or preceding actions were similar but also those in which the acting person thought of a preceding or subsequent action when committing the error. But any precise recording of such thoughts is out of the question because of the transient nature of these phenomena. It should furthermore be taken into regard that not only actions carried out a short time or directly before, or carried out a short time after or directly after, an action can have a previous or an aftereffect and that it is hardly possible to trace all actions lying farther back or ahead. And even if this were possible it could hardly be assessed whether these past or future actions did exercise any real influence or not. Because of these deficiencies it will have to be assumed that the negative percentage of my cases is too high and the positive one too low.

Since perseveration and anticipation are not the only determining factors in the substitutions but other elements also seem to play a role, a competition may develop between the various factors, and that factor will gain the upper hand which will have been the more determining one in the respective case. This may entail the interesting fact that in a few cases it is precisely the rarer action which gradually develops into the determining factor. Since the investigated actions repeat themselves on a daily basis it is not possible to compile precise statistics on those cases where the rarer objects, places and movements are replacing the more frequent ones. As a result of different attendant circumstances, the rarer action gained the upper hand over the more frequent one in 58 cases of my collection of substitutions.

Examples of substitutions in which the rarer instead of the more frequent action was carried out: I (no. 24) put the lid of the dirty water tub on the jug where it is never placed; take the gray, more rarely used, instead of the red, more frequently used, notebook into my hand (no. 173); take a dish with fat, which I reach for on rarer occasions, instead of the spirit burner ,into the kitchen (no. 272); instead of the writing pen box I reach for the toothpick box, which is taken out more rarely to be refilled (no. 342); hang the flyswatter, instead of on its nail, on a nail on the opposite wall for which I reach more rarely (nos. 444, 446, 616, 617); I seize the writing desk drawer, which was taken out upside down in order to put it back, although this upside down movement has never occurred (no. 503); In order to cut bread A., instead of reaching for the knife, reaches for the hatchet, which she only rarely had in her hands (no. 637); instead of using the outside toilet, which is used several times a day, she goes to the stable where she has been only three or four times a year (no. 795); in order to lift the stove cover she reaches for the briquette tongs, which she has not used for years, instead of the iron rod which is to be used for this purpose (no. 854) etc. In all of these cases the erroneously chosen object or place was nearer, more convenient, or directly in front of one's eyes or hands.

The law of the fastened and ended melody is a special case of the perseverative mental set and in this study is meant to include those perseverations in which the parts of a multi-part action which have once been experienced in this order will occur in the same order if the first parts of the action occur again.

Examples of the law of the linked and completed sequence: A. (no. 98) dices bread in order to toast it. After one cup is full of bread cubes, that is to say, after she has repeated the cutting movement about twenty to thirty times, she wants to cut a few big slices of bread to toast them, but she has come into such full cutting swing that she dices more pieces of bread instead of cutting big slices. A. (no. 334) repeatedly throws waste into the stove but then reaches for a floor cloth lying underneath the waste, instead of the waste, and throws the cloth into the fire.

In cases 294, 395, 489, 647, 718, 709, 785, 1003, 1007, 1041, 1062, 10073, 1095, both principal subjects (A. and J.) carry two to three objects into the pantry, objects which should be put on different racks and shelves. After one object had been put in its proper place, the movement, which had come into full swing, caused the other objects to be put in the place where the first and second object had been placed instead of their proper place.

The reader will find quite a large number of examples of Weimer's subsequent errors among the specified substitutions. The same factor which is an original error in the first case will develop into a subsequent error in the repetitions by perseveration. If, for example, in case 9 J. dips his pen into the teacup instead of the inkpot, this is an original error, whereas the same substitution has turned into a perseverative subsequent error in case 10.

The mental set also includes the affect and the associated value or interest problem. When assessing this problem it is advisable to refrain from devoting oneself to fussy interpretation skills, which observers endowed with too much imagination might tend to use.

If, for example, I am placing my spectacles into the purse for small change instead of the brown case, the side-by-side location of both objects on the table, their dark color and their function, but not a secret worshipping of money (in this case of small change?), are the reasons for the substitution (no. 1). In the same way, the confusion of the thermometer with the picture of Christ cannot be interpreted as a symptom of being emotionally tied to the Savior when the location of both objects on the wall, and the fact that the thermometer was previously hanging above the picture, are enough reason for the confusion. The genital symbols, this only embodiment of the soul according to classical psychoanalysis, could never be of any importance in my collection. As far as the interest and value problem is concerned, the statement must be made that the erroneous action is always simply negative in terms of value; it must be repaired if the acting person wants to achieve his or her goal. In a few cases, however, a temporarily higher interest[19] may exist in favor of the erroneous action. This primarily applies to the combined cases, where not just the elements of the action but the entire action is mixed up. But this is not true for all

---

[19] See also Kollarits, *Das momentane Interesse bei nervösen und nicht nervösen Menschen*. J. f. Psychol. u. Neur. **21** (1915).

such cases.

If A. presents me with a thread torn off a carpet instead of the requested notebook (no. 871), this process of grasping the thread shows the housewife's temporarily higher interest in order and cleanliness than in the request. As far as the purpose of the action is concerned, the second part of the action, which involves the very substitution, however, constitutes a loss in value. If I am distracted from my action by a wasp at the window and therefore kill it, the temporary interest in the execution job is stronger than in the intended action, but it constitutes a loss in value for the action. There are only five cases in my entire collection which certainly belong here.

My collection does not include an affect-related case, i.e. a case where the wrong action would have replaced the right one for merely affective reasons, unless the cases which have been discussed, and in which distraction has given the illusion of a temporarily different aspect of interest, are intended to be counted among the affective substitutions. Although the interest in an action can be associated with an affect, we do not want to rate interest and affect as being identical. This does not mean that an affect cannot cause a substitution in such a way that instead of the necessary, but not pleasure-orientated, action a pleasure-orientated one will follow; or that, based on this, a more pleasure-orientated but more incorrect object or place could be substituted for the displeasure-orientated one, or even vice-versa. Although my collection of 742 substitutions does not include such a case it does not follow therefrom that relatively rare cases like those may not happen in a very large number e.g. 10 000, of substitutions. In this connection I recall my work on writing errors where I found just one affective error among 1007 other ones. Here, the wrong word "Muret" has replaced the word "thoughtlessness", that is to say, out of annoyance and not out of a pleasure orientation, the name of Mr. Maurice Muret, the enemy of the Germans and Hungarians, the daily writer of the Gazette de Lausanne, who filled the columns of this paper with his malicious, defamatory rubbish. It is interesting in this case that, apart from the number of syllables there was no similarity between the words exchanged for one another, neither in the sound of the words nor in their meanings. The name seemed to have been completely latent within myself and suddenly came into my mind like an intermediary idea[20], which I then used in my writing. It is as important to note that not a pleasure-orientated but a displeasure-orientated word replaced the correct one.

But the substitutions also entail another aspect of the problem of affect, and of the problems of value and interest as well. I have said that

---

[20] Kollarits, Der plötzliche Einfall. Umschau **1918**, Nr. 23, and more detailed in Hungarian: Intermediärer Einfall u. Erinnerung. Term. tud. Közlöny, vol. 50.

the ego is split away from the performance of a task if errors occur. The splitting away may happen when one's full attention is directed towards the purpose but one does not pursue the process of implementation. If I dip my pen into the tea instead of the ink, the ego is not split away from the purpose, the thought, but only from the mechanical action. But it is also possible that such a mechanical action is performed incorrectly because I think of something completely different from the purpose, even if the purpose is more pleasure-orientated than the performance of the task or the foreign thought is more pleasure-orientated than the respective purpose. The pleasure and displeasure orientation affects the splitting away of the ego from the respective task but not the object, place or movement of the error which has replaced the correct action.

I count the misleading substitutions among the mental set errors where, for example, the unexpected position of a lock, bolt, handle or door leads to the opposite erroneous movement.

Examples of misleading substitutions: The window knob that should be shut is not bolted. In fact, I notice the direction of the bolt and ought to conclude that the window opens without turning this knob. Although I knows this theoretically I virtually do not take any notice of it, and because I go to the window with my mind set on the fact that the knob is bolted and should be turned, I make the only possible movement, by which the window is bolted. Then I rattle at the window and become annoyed without noticing that I have bolted the window (no. 26). I had forgotten to bolt a door. It is true that I notice the position of the bolt but because I approached the bolt with my mind set on the idea that the bolt is locked and must be pulled I make the only possible movement under these circumstances, i.e. I lock the bolt. Then I rattle at the door with all my might, without knowing at the moment why it cannot be opened, before I notice my mistake.

If different mental set errors are made at the same time, it can often hardly be established why one is stronger in this case, and why the other is stronger in that case.

The calculation of the mental set factors results in the following statistics. In 742 substitutions the following could be established:

mental set factors in 647 cases = 87.20 %
no mental set factors in 95 cases = 12.80%
all mental set factors in 742 cases = 100%

But it has also to be borne in mind here that a mental set factor may go unnoticed due to the transitory character of the phenomenon, whereas the opposite case, i.e. the erroneous assumption of a mental set factor, does not occur. The percentage of 87 for the existence of the mental set factors will thus be too high and the percentage of 13 for the absence of these factors too low. But one thing is certain, namely that the mental set factor is of importance in the vast majority of the substitutions.

It can now be ascertained in the substitutions without mental set factors why the incorrect objects, places and movements were selected out of two correct objects, places and movements when the intention was barred. According to the calculation of probability the same situation should lead to 50 % of substitutions and 50 % of successes. If I am standing, for example, in front of a lock and the key is in the lock, and if I turn the key while the intention is barred, half of the turns should theoretically lock and half of the turns should open the lock. The same percentage of errors should theoretically be produced if two similar or dissimilar objects are lying at the same distance in front of me, and I reach for one of these objects without looking at them -- which happens often when the attention is diverted. The 50 % of those cases where one reaches for the correct object under these circumstances certainly do not count, if only the errors are recorded.

The Hamiltonian principle of the expenditure of least energy applies not only to the 13.2 % of substitutions without mental set factors, where it is the primary reason in addition to the splitting away of the ego and similarity, but also to the substitutions with mental set factors, where it is a concomitant factor. This principle facilitates the similarity attraction. As far as the substitutions are concerned, it has the effect that the action will be curtailed or otherwise facilitated and, figuratively speaking, will lead to a short circuit. This principle can be found in choosing a distance where the shorter distance takes precedence over the longer one, the straight line over the bent one and the lesser leverage over the higher one. But here different factors are competing with the Hamiltonian principle, perseveration and anticipation, the assimilation processes of homogeneity, the mental sets which are stronger and are able to push the law of the expenditure of least energy into the background. Since I became aware of this fact only after a very long time of observation and did, therefore, not always put down the respective information, I am not able to compile any statistics on the percentage of cases in which the technically easier performance of work gained the upper hand over the technically more difficult one. At least, this fact could frequently be established at a later date.

Examples of the precedence of the shorter distance: The cupboard out of which J. is erroneously taking out the cotton wool is closer to me than the washstand in whose drawer the cotton wool is lying (no. 13) The wrong switch is closer than the right one (no. 27); the teacup erroneously reached for is closer than the desired match box (no. 165), the more rarely used gray notebook closer than the more often used red one (no. 173), the nail on which the scarf was erroneously hung was closer than the right one, the sponge erroneously reached for closer than the soap (no. 1009), the handkerchief in the resting left hand closer than (the working right hand is not to be used here), the blotting paper etc..

Examples of the precedence of movement along a straight line over that along a bent line: The wrong way to the kitchen is a straight one, the right one would entail a turn around a bend (nos. 129, 294). The wrong shelf is straight on, whereas the right one would require a turn (no 169). The way to the anteroom to which the rice was erroneously taken is a straight one, whereas the right way to the pantry requires a turn (no. 220) etc..

The saving of energy during lifting comes into play in all those cases where an object is put on the lower shelf instead of the right one, e.g. in cases 163, 167, 191, 228, 265, 275 etc.

If several factors are acting at the same time, all these facilitating procedures are competing with the other factors and, if necessary, will recede into the background. Here, the mechanically more difficult way has become the psychologically easier one, due to the interference of the other factors.

Examples of a competition between various factors in which the action which is easier in mechanical terms makes way for the psychologically easier one. A chocolate box is often placed one shelf higher than required because some time ago it stood on the higher shelf. J. erroneously goes to the table which is farther away instead of the stove, because he more frequently goes to the stove than to this table (no. 16). It was easier in this case to take the longer, but "established" way than to take the shorter unusual one. J. is erroneously throwing the stamps into the wastepaper basket standing farther away instead of putting them into the nearer drawer, because he had just thrown waste paper into the wastepaper basket. Perseveration thus makes the repetition of the same movement easier than the adjustment[21] to another movement which is shorter and, apart from the circumstances described, requires a lesser expenditure of energy in mechanical terms.

---

[21] For more information on adjustments see Marbe, Zsch. f. angew. Psychol. **26** (1926), Archiv für Psychologie, vol. 99.

4 The Omissions

Out of the 206 (18.72 %) of the omissions in my collection 128 were caused by me, 64 by Anna, and 4 by other subjects occasionally observed. It is out of the question to atomize the omissions into object, place, and mere movement omissions, since any omission affects the object, the place and the movement in the same way, which makes the question much easier. So, every single action is a part in a series of successive actions. In accordance with the experience gained in our substitutions, and in the known writing, speaking and reading errors as well, these series have to be reviewed, and it has to be found out whether the respective series includes partially identical parts before and after the omission. These parts must also be reviewed for the homogeneity of the elements, of the objects, places and of the mere movements. Here, the conditions frequently differ from those of the substitutions. As far as the substitutions are concerned, we have primarily reviewed the similarity of the elements confused with one another and hardly checked the non-confused elements for their identity or partial identity, since those non-confused elements had hardly any effect as to whether these very objects, places or movements of all others had been confused. When I go from one room to another room which is the wrong choice, the partially identical element of the action, the process of walking, does not affect my confusion of one place with another; just so, in the wrong action of dipping the pen into the tea instead of the ink, it is neither the process of dipping, nor the pen reached for, that is the determining factor in confusing the tea with the ink, but the partial identity of both liquids. But a comparison of the omitted action and the preceding and subsequent parts in the omissions produces both partial identities and identities of all elements.

Table 4: Statistics of Omissions

		Subject J.				Subject A.				S+M	All subjects			
		no.	%	no.	%	no.	%	no.	%	no.	no.	%	no.	%
Fully homogeneous	In preceding and subsequent parts	96	69.57	115	83.34	52	81.25	60	93.75	3	151	73.3	178	86.41
	In preceding parts	15	10.87			6	9.38			-	21	10.19		
	In subsequent parts	4	2.90			2	3.14			-	6	2.91		
1-2 heterogeneous parts with homogenous totality characteristics	In preceding and subsequent parts	19	13.77	22	15.94	1	1.56	1	1.56	1	21	10.19	24	10.65
	In preceding parts	3	2.17			-	-	-	-	-	3	1.46		
Heterogeneous		1	0.72	1	0.72	3	4.69	3	4.69		4	1.94	4	1.94
Total		138	100	138	100	64	100	64	100	4	206	99.99	206	100

Table 4 shows the statistics of the omissions of my collection. It compares for homogeneity both the parts implemented before and those after the omission, with the omitted part. Here we found homogeneity before or after the omission, or both before and after. It is not so easy as in the speaking, reading and writing errors to determine which of the actions carried out before or after the omitted action should be taken into consideration. If a character, e.g. an e, was omitted in reading or writing we will attribute this error only to identical letters appearing in close proximity to the omitted character and not to those which appeared a long time before or which will appear a long time later. In the routine everyday actions, however, all identical actions occurring throughout the day may have an influence. If I, for example, want to open my window which has two latches on each wing, and I forget to open one of the latches, the opening of the first latch is considered to be a preceding part in the action. After a few minutes I close the window with two latches, having reached for two similar objects, an identical and a partially identical one, and carried out two movements showing a partial identity of the opposite in contrast to the process of opening. The question is now how far in the future similarity should be anticipated and how far back in the past it should be traced. Although it is certain that the daily repeated actions constitute an almost continuous flow of actions (putting one's clothes on and off, washing oneself, making the beds, cooking meals, cleaning) which are influencing one another, when assessing homogeneity I restricted myself on the similarities occurring in the course of the same day.

We also have omissions which possess dissimilar elements in the preceding and subsequent parts of the series which, however, when considered in their entirety possess similar characteristics in this entirety. Finally, we also have omissions in whose preceding and subsequent parts we did not find any similar element even from the most general point of view and which were thus completely heterogeneous.

In the omissions of the two main subjects we found significant discrepancies which might be explained by differences in the respective personalities but would perhaps be compensated for in a larger number of cases. Discrepancies may, however, also arise from the subjects' different ways of living, depending on whether a person has to cope with more or less similar series of actions in his or her daily routine. A housewife who, for example, only exercises a supervisory function in her household escapes the similar omissions which occur when the beds are made, the table is set, rooms are cleared up etc.

Much agreement is to be found if we compare the statistics of omissions with those of substitutions. The highest percentages are reached by the homogeneous errors for both types of errors; for the substitutions the percentage is 90.05 and for the omissions 86.41 %. These are followed by those heterogeneous errors which, considered in their entire environment, have similar characteristics in this entirety. Their percentage is 8.38 for the substitutions and 10.65 % for the omissions. In both cases the completely heterogeneous errors have the lowest percentage, 0.40 for the substitutions and 1.94 % for the omissions. What matters in this comparison are not differences of several percent and also not absolute percentages but, in the first place the order, and in the second the large intervals in the order of substitutions or omissions.

Examples of omissions occurring between completely similar preceding and subsequent parts of a series: One of my daily repeated actions is to take sheets, blankets and pillows from my divan bed to another room. After shaking out these bed utensils from the window, I pass them on to Anna in a certain order, and she stores them in the empty bed. Then I pass on the decorated pillow-case and a fancy pillow. During the ten months when the errors were recorded, the procedure was repeated around 300 times. In 29 of these cases, that is in around 10 % of the cases, I omitted one of the nine bed utensils, in fact, mostly one of the last utensils. All those objects are partially identical as bed utensils, the passing on of the objects as a movement and the places where they were taken from and placed on are identical. Another weekly repetitive action is my shaving myself with a razor. In the 43 shaving procedures, nine actions (21 %) were omitted in the course of the observation period: on five occasions it was forgotten to close the blade, on two occasions to put it back into its box and on one occasion to insert the grid into the razor. The omissions are preceded by a number of actions involving the razor or its components: taking the razor and sharpener out of the drawer, taking the equipment out of their boxes etc.. These are partially identical objects, places and movements. There are more partially identical subsequent parts of a series of actions to follow, depending on which part was omitted; these are several actions concerning the assembly of the razor, the process of shaving, the cleaning of the razor components, their disassembly and stowing away in the boxes and in the drawer. In the course of opening the window, which has two latches on each wing, I forgot to open one of the latches, and, always the second one, on eleven occasions. Here, the opening of the first latch as a preceding part of the series of actions is partially identical, and, after the room has been aired and the window shut, the closing of the latches constitutes a partial identity of the opposite. The partial identity of the preceding part and also of the subsequent parts of the series of actions is, however, a determining factor for the omission. Analogously to these omissions I forgot to bolt the door of the outside toilet from the inside with the second latch on six occasions. Here, the bolting of the first latch is the preceding similar part of the series of actions, whereas the processes of opening the two latches follow as partially identical subsequent parts of the action series. That the described function of the double bolt is learned in the course of time is shown by the fact that these errors no longer occur in cases 443 to 1100, when the same latches are opened and closed several times a day.

Another daily repetitive serial action is putting on one's clothes where omissions can occur and where a number of objects are reached for and put on in a certain order, objects which are partially identical as pieces of clothing and which are taken from partially identical places and put on partially identical parts of the body by using partially identical movements. An omission of the medium part of a series is thus preceded by the omission of partially identical parts of the action. Such cases are, for example, forgetting to pull the tie through the collar (no. 561), to put on elastic stockings (no. 499), to knot the tie (no. 1022), to put on one's shirt (no. 950), to put on the makeup cape (no. 976) etc. A common-place omission is forgetting to button up one's trousers where mostly the unbuttoning and the different processes of unbuttoning and buttoning up articles of clothing during the day constitute the similar preceding and subsequent parts of the action series. - Kitchen work can also cause similar omissions, particularly when various ingredients must be added one after the other to a dish or to several simultaneously prepared dishes; these ingredients constitute similar preceding and subsequent parts of the action series in which case the places of the action and the movements are also partially identical. In one case it was forgotten to add grated lemon peel (no, 722), in another case parsley (no. 305), and in a third case garlic (no. 396), since the cooking procedure required the addition of several different ingredients before and after the omission. I have three cases (nos. 252, 292, 565) in my collection where the lesser separation function, as a preceding part of the action series, created a similar inhibition of the major one, and the similar subsequent parts of the action series were included in the similar daily functions.

Examples of omissions initiated by similar preceding parts of action series. In the evening A. carries a glass into the kitchen and forgets to take the respective saucer with her. The similar preceding part of the action series is that the glass and its saucer have previously been brought into the room. Since no more glasses and cups are moved around the same evening, we do not assume any similar subsequent part of the action series (no. 266). A. puts sugar on one cake and forgets to put sugar on the second one. Putting sugar on the first cake is the similar preceding part of the action series. A similar subsequent part of the action series does not exist.

Examples of omissions without similar preceding parts but with similar subsequent parts of the action series. In the morning J. begins with putting on his clothes by first reaching for his trousers, thus omitting his stockings and underpants (nos. 35, 60). Since he did not have anything to do with an article of clothing before he started to put on his clothes ,the omission was not preceded by a similar preceding part of the action series, but it is followed by a succession of similar subsequent parts of the action series when putting on more articles of clothing. In the morning A. forgets to put on the first article of clothing, the elastic stockings. A similar preceding part of the action series does not exist, but a whole series of actions involving the putting on of clothes is to follow; these are similar subsequent parts of the action series.

Examples of omissions where the omitted object is heterogeneous as against the objects of the preceding and subsequent parts of the action series but the entire action includes homogeneous environmental characteristics. J. carries his writing utensils from his room to the verandah but forgets the floor lamp which he also needs because it will soon become dark. The floor lamp is heterogeneous as compared to the other writing utensils: ink, pen, briefcase, notes, writing paper, but under the aspect of the entirety of the writing utensils to be used in the evening, the floor lamp also belongs to the writing utensils (no. 822). He is looking for a receipt in his writing desk drawer, clears out the entire drawer for this purpose and puts the objects found on the table: receipts, a photocopy frame, notes, toothpick and writing pen boxes, an ear trumpet, a plexor, an envelope with vignettes. Upon finding the receipt looked for, he puts back all specified objects but forgets the photocopy frame on the table. The photocopy frame is heterogeneous in itself and with respect to the other specified objects. From the aspect of its entirety, i.e. its location in the same drawer, its environment is, however, similar. To prove that this similarity is not "far-fetched" it can be said that only the joint location in the drawer implies that the objects belong together; without this belongingness, the photocopy frame could not have been omitted when the objects were put back into the drawer (nos 78, 468, 734). The location and the movement itself are also similar. A cloth and a water jug are in themselves as dissimilar as possible. But if I carry a water jug from the kitchen to my room I always put a cloth underneath the jug in order that the dripping water might not wet the floor. But I forgot the cloth on two occasions (nos. 553 and 946). As far as the object is concerned, the omission of the cloth during the action would constitute a heterogeneous omission. But in this special case the cloth and the jug belong together as component parts of a complex whole, that is to say they have similar characteristics in this complex whole. The location of the action and the carrying of the objects as a movement are identical.

The heterogeneous omissions. All of the four omissions are specified here, because they are of special interest: In the pantry J. catches sight of a wasp and intends to go to the kitchen to get the flyswatter in order to play the role of an executioner. Meanwhile, he is called away, whereupon he leaves the pantry and forgets his plan. Catching sight of the wasp was not preceded by an action which could, in any way, have constituted a homogeneous inhibition. After the omission a conversation took place which was also in no way associated with the forgotten action (no. 658). (The case is not identical with case no. 627, a dissimilarity-based substitution, where the wasp was killed, and it is not to be confused with it.) On two successive occasions A. leaves the kitchen where she cultivates her culinary talents to go into her room in order to get her sewing things, and in both cases, returns to the kitchen without having achieved anything and continues her kitchen work which does not have any characteristics similar to the sewing things. In case 677 A. is also making preparations for sewing but forgets it completely after the cleaning woman has asked her a question that takes her to a different household world. In all these omissions the omission occurred as a result of distraction by completely dissimilar trains of thought and actions.

As in the substitutions, we also find quite a large number of errors in the omissions where Ranschburg's homogeneous attraction is not only included but is also a conscious element of the experience.

Examples of similarity attractions as conscious elements of the experience. On one occasion J. omits the putting on of his stockings, and on another occasion the putting on of the stockings and the underpants by reaching for the trousers as a first movement in the process of putting on his clothes and realizing the error after having carried out the wrong movement. The similarity attraction manifests itself in the glance thrown at, and in the reach for, the trousers (nos. 35 and 60). In the longer, completely similar series, e.g. in arranging the nine similar bed utensils that I have talked about, it is often the glance which skims over the respective object before it comes next and which induces the wrong reach. The attraction of a train of thought can also often come into play when the thoughts are concentrated on the subsequent parts of the series by producing a visual image of this object. The case can be considered to be analogous to those writing errors where the silent dictation given to oneself anticipates the letter in visual or language terms and, therefore, the letter is put down. In some cases of the longer series, as for example in handling the razor, this might be called a grasping attraction when a wrong component of the razor almost falls into one's hands.

In the omissions, several aspects of the suppression of differences come into play. First of all, differences are already suppressed in all omissions, because the omitted part is never fully but only partially identical, since partial identity is not full identity; that is to say it includes not only identical but also differing characteristics. In these cases, the suppression of the differing characteristic is always initiated by the homogeneous attraction in addition to the amalgamation with the identical part of the action series. When one of the utensils belonging to the bed is omitted, for example the gray blanket, and also the previously spread linen sheet and the following blue blanket etc. are partially identical, i.e. identical as bed utensils, identical in their shape and size; but they are also differing in color, in the quality of the fabrics etc. Also the place of the action is partially identical and at the same time partially differing, since, when the individual objects were reached for, they were lying side by side and not in exactly the same place, and they were partly lying side by side and partly one upon the other.

The suppression of differences is even more conspicuous in those omissions where the omitted objects are in themselves heterogeneous and only include homogeneous characteristics in their entirety. For all that, the similarity-based inhibition seems to be the dominant factor also in those omissions which occurred as a result of the amalgamation. In that case, for example, in which different heterogeneous objects had been put in and out of the drawer and the dissimilar photocopy frame had been forgotten when the objects were put back, the error was not caused by the dissimilar part of the action series itself but by the similar characteristic of its complex wholes.

The suppression of differences is particularly obvious in those omissions which were embedded in a completely dissimilar action environment. These cases were not governed by the homogeneous attraction but by the heterogeneous abstraction, i.e. distraction. In two of these four cases the persons committing the errors were distracted by other persons in their planning. In the two remaining cases the distraction was caused by trains of thought which turned to other tasks.

When we dealt with the substitutions, we made the statement that the splitting away of the ego from the intended action can also constitute a suppression of differences. In the omissions this suppression of differences acts as the dominant factor determining that an error is occurring, whereas the homogeneous inhibition determines which objects, places or movements are included in the error. There will be some among the readers who might doubt whether the similarity-based inhibition has any influence whatsoever on the error; whether for example the blue blanket was really omitted because it was preceded by linen sheets and other blankets and followed by another blanket. I think that I can answer this question by using statistics. If the homogeneous inhibition were not important, my collection would not include 86.41 % fully homogeneous, 10.65 % omissions which are homogeneous in their overall situation and only 1.94 % fully heterogeneous omissions.

We have said that the homogeneous inhibition is the determining factor for the elements of an action or the actions which are to be included in an error. But we still do not know why, after the splitting away of the same intention and through the same homogeneous inhibition, a substitution is caused on one occasion and an omission on another. It should first be considered whether each omission might constitute a substitution which would blur the difference between a substitution and an omission. We have already answered this question in so far as this view can only be assumed for a few, but not for all, cases. Are the outward circumstances the determining factor to answer the question whether the error is to develop into an omission or a substitution under the otherwise same conditions of dissimilarity?

A few observations show that the outward circumstances play a certain role. If I want, for example, to reach for the pen to put down what I am reading, and while doing this continue reading, do not look at the writing desk, grope for the pen and then a pencil lying closer to me comes into my hands instead of the pen, it can easily happen that, while I am still absorbed in the book, I dip the pencil into the ink without looking at it. It can happen under the same conditions that I dip the penholder into the ink when the pen was lying upside down or that I, without looking, dip the pen into the tea. If, in the cases described, the pencil had not been lying there, if the penholder of the pen had not been lying in my direction, if the teacup had not been standing beside the inkpot no error would have been made. Furthermore, the upside down position of the pen, the position of the pencil and the teacup could not have "occasioned" an omission but only a substitution. "Occasion" is the correct expression since it is only the occasion which was provided by the outward circumstances, the latter of which only play a secondary role, for the splitting away of the intention would have to be a different one if the same circumstances had not produced a substitution but an omission. An omission could quite well happen, even if a pencil had replaced the pen, and irrespective of whether the pen had been lying in the correct or upside down position, or whether the teacup would have been standing beside the inkpot or not. If we now review how the intention is split away in substitutions and omissions, we will come across quite a few differences. Let us, for example, take the simple case where the flyswatter has always been hung on the nail on the opposite wall instead of the proper nail. In this case, the intention exists to such a degree that the correct object is reached for, the correct movement of hanging is carried out, and even to that degree that the place "a nail in the wall" is chosen correctly. The splitting away is thus only concentrated on a minor point, on such a point that the position of the nail on another wall is not recognized. Such a small degree of the intention being split away from the action can only occasion a substitution but not an omission since an omission can only be caused when the splitting away of the intention would affect the entire action of hanging up an object or even more. It can, for example, be forgotten actually to take the flyswatter into one's hands and hang it up. If the splitting away of the intention from the action does not reach such a stage, that is to say if the murderous weapon has been taken into one's hands, an omission could still occur, because it is kept in one's hands but nothing is done with it. As soon, however, as it is no longer in one's hands and is put down on the table, this very action is a substitution and not an omission, since the act of hanging an object on the nail has been replaced by the act of putting an object down on the table. The same trains of thought also apply to the cases involving the pen and the pencil in which the omission could only have affected the entire action.

The reader is requested to rethink the analysis himself by using the example of the flyswatter. This would, in the majority of cases, be a certain explanation of these phenomena but not an exhaustive one, since in the cases discussed under this aspect up to now, the difference between an omission and a substitution is not only lying in the fact that, as far as omissions are concerned, the splitting away of the intention from the action covers all elements of the action but, as far as substitutions are concerned, this is true not only for parts of the elements, but also in the fact that in this stage, a correct object is replaced by a wrong one. This replacement of the correct object by the wrong one can, as we have seen, have been caused by outward circumstances, but if I read my watch instead of the thermometer, the outward circumstances have not caused this substitution to happen but rather a wrong mental set. Here, the intention is not only split away from the purpose in one stage of the action, but there is an additional advantage in this stage, namely that the correct object is replaced by a wrong one. We come back to the topic which has already been discussed, namely that the substitution is an omission + an insertion.

When we talked about the splitting away of the intention in a small segment of the action, we used the expression: "in cases dealt with up to now under this aspect". Now, we turn to those cases which have not been dealt with up to now under this aspect, that is to say, to the comparison of the intention in those cases where the error extends to the entire action, namely to all elements of the action, not only in the omissions but also in the substitutions. These cases in my collection are homogeneous in all elements. By mere accident there are two cases which are particularly favorable for comparison purposes, one substitution and one omission and which I will analyze here. These are the two "wasp cases", no. 627 as the substitution and no. 658 as the omission. In the first case, the lazy fellow's being lured out of the room to the verandah was substituted by the killing of the wasp, in the second case the erring person was called away when he was about to kill a wasp in the pantry, so that his plan was not substituted by another action. Here, we have no longer to deal with the difference that in one case the intention has been split away through all stages and in another case in only one stage of the action. Instead, we are confronted with the following difference in the intention: in the first case, the ego turns to another action because of the homogeneity, in the second case, it remains passive as far as an action is possible if it is not intended to take the implementation of the omission, i.e. leaving the place of the action, into consideration and rename the omission to become a substitution. Also in this case of a dissimilarity-based substitution we are thus confronted with the same phenomenon in all elements, as in the substitution of one element, namely that the substitution is an omission + an insertion, but that the omission is a mere omission.

The differentiation between an omission and a confusion, or in more correct terms, a substitution, however, becomes relatively uncertain if it is assumed that the person who has been distracted from his plans by external influences will do something else even if he merely listens to a question asked by another person and answers it. It would be necessary here to expand the collection of material about completely heterogeneous omissions and completely heterogeneous substitutions to investigate the question in more detail. In the pure omission which concerns all elements of the action, that is to say the entire action, the intention would be split away from the planned action whereas, in the substitutions, it would not only be split away from two entire actions which concern all elements but would also search for new purposes.

In the beginning of this work we said that the omission must be a technically more serious error than the substitution, since resistance against the error happening is greater in the former case. This is true for most errors of both categories insofar as the omission suspends the whole action but the substitution only one or two elements of it. In those cases where two completely homogeneous actions are completely, i.e. in all elements, confused with one another or omitted, this difference does not apply. But in addition to others, these cases constitute a trivially small minority, that is to say 1.94 % in my omissions and 0.40 % in my substitutions.

2. The Mental Set

Since most omissions are daily repetitive actions, it cannot be excluded that the actions carried out during other days also have a retroactive or anticipatory effect. But in order not to attribute a too far-reaching effect to perseveration and anticipation, I have also restricted this aspect to the same day. Perhaps the limits set for the effects of both factors are too narrow on the one hand, but, on the other hand, they are too far-reaching, since it is possible but not certain and, at least, difficult to judge, whether there is interaction, mutual inhibition or support between two actions separated by a time interval of one or several hours. The substitutions did not confront us with this difficult question since the confused actions or the confused elements of the action are simultaneous.

As far as the substitutions are concerned, we have endorsed those authors' views who consider the anticipation to be a variety of perseveration. In the omissions contained in our collection, the difference between the two factors is of a technical nature only, since the last actions of the day cannot entail any subsequent parts and the penultimate actions only a few subsequent parts of the action, and since the first actions of the day do not include any preceding parts of the action which could have had anticipatory or more perseverative effects.

In the omissions, that kind of perseveration that I count among those under the law of the commenced sequence can only belong to the so-called subsequent errors of Weimers, where the omission, once having occurred, causes the error to be repeated. In these cases, the situation is as follows: If a note has been omitted from a sequence by mistake there is a tendency that this note is also omitted when the sequence is reeled off again. If, thus, a, b, d, e was played instead of a, b, c, d, e it can happen that the wrong sequence is continued on the second stroke of a, b. This reminds us of the bad female piano players in the neighboring flat, of whom we know in advance that they will produce the same mistakes even in the hundredth repetition of the same opus. The momentum of the wrong melody to which they have become accustomed overwhelms the once omitted note in the same way as the wrong note suppresses the correct one.

Example of omissions on the basis of the commenced melody. In case 310 and thereafter in case 312, J forgot to open the second door bolt; he went twice from the verandah into the room to collect his gloves but returned the first and the second time without having collected the gloves (nos. 327, 328); forgot on two successive occasions to open the second window latch after the first one (nos. 716, 717); forgot to put the library collection slip into the book parcel when the books are sent back, became aware of the omission, unpacked the books, put them back into the parcel and forgot for the second time to put the collection slip into the parcel.

In my collection of omissions, the affect problem is not reflected in such a way that the omitted part of the action series would have a special displeasure orientation. For example if out of nine similar blankets, linen sheets, and pillows used as bed utensils the gray blanket is omitted on one occasion and the blue one on another occasion, this does not mean that the gray or the blue blanket is displeasure-orientated. The truth is that the whole action series is boring for the respective subject, that is to say displeasure-orientated since he is of the opinion that he could have done something more sensible if the conditions of his life had been better. This displeasure orientation contributes to the fact that a part of the series is omitted. The decision as to which part is to be omitted depends on the pleasure orientation only insofar as the subject becomes more readily impatient with the last parts of the ordeal and therefore tends to omit, almost always, one of the last parts of the action. This is not supposed to mean that there might not be a case where the omitted part is detested. But this must be a relatively rare case when it is not to be found among 206 cases. And it can also not be held true for most cases that the part of the action series following the omitted part, for example that after the omission of the seventh object which belongs to the bed, in this case the very eighth object, should be attributed a special pleasure orientation. In the same way, the forgotten process of sharpening the razor blade is not displeasure-orientated and the next part of the action series, the insertion of the grid into the razor, is not particularly pleasure-orientated. The value and interest problem associated with the affect may, however, apply in a few rare cases insofar as the present interest turns to that action or those trains of thought that follow the omission.

Since perseveration and anticipation are mental set factors, and since they are effective in 86.41 % of my collection of omissions in the preceding or subsequent part or in both parts of the action series and, furthermore, since also the dissimilar parts in the complex whole have similar components in 10.65 % of my collection and, furthermore, since in the remaining four cases (1.94 %) of the heterogeneous **distraction** is the determining element which is also a mental set, a mental set factor is more or less effective in 100 % of the cases. The mental set, thus, seems to play an even more important role in the omissions than in the substitutions, where we were able to establish 48% for the negative cases with complete certainty but certain reservations.

Since the omission constitutes a shortcut, so to speak, a short circuit, with regard to the ultimate goal, the Hamiltonian principle of the expenditure of least energy comes into play, which means that the mechanical principle without pursuing the proper goal acts freely in the apparatus which has lost its pilot after the very intention has been eliminated. In reaching for the subsequent object of the series, the same principle will then apply when the nearer, but not directly following, object is grasped.

JENÖ KOLLARITS

5 Insertions

Our collection includes 133 foreign insertions of which 83 are from myself, 49 from Anna and one from subject Gy.

1. Attraction factors

Before we assess the role which attraction factors might play in insertions, we shall first examine without prejudice whether these insertions share identical or partially identical characteristics with certain other actions of the same person.

In some cases, the insertion is the repetition of a habitual action of a series that has been induced by the preceding part in the series. It certainly happened to everyone that at the moment of leaving or entering a room in the daytime was about to switch on or off the electric light as he was accustomed to do in the evening. The action induced this way is identical to the habitual action. Such cases of insertions partly correspond to the repetitions discussed in the next chapter, since they are also repetitions; but they differ from those repetitions in that the latter refer to the repetition of an immediately preceding action. Since such habitual series of actions must be repeated in the same order in future as well, this type of insertion has, in addition to a perseverative, an anticipatory component which, however, plays a minor role and is still based on the past. In contrast to these insertions, the action inserted in other cases is not an exact copy of the immediately preceding action, because, although it is performed with the same object, the place and motion of the second, i.e. the inserted, action differs from those of the first action in that they have an opposite direction: the object has been taken from one place to another and then unnecessarily been taken back to the first place.

The examples given below will convince any doubters that these cases are not to be classified as interpretations as it might seem at first. On taking the object from one place to another, the person committing an error had not intended to carry out any action which he then forgot, i.e. omitted. The immediately successive actions also include cases in which the same action is not repeated with the same object but with another one, while the entire repetition constitutes an insertion of an unnecessary or even inappropriate action. The object of this action and the object of the preceding action can be partially identical or dissimilar.

Since every action considered in our cases is carried out with an object at a place and consists in a movement, both an insertion and an omission can only refer to an entire action and not, as it is possible in cases of substitution, to individual elements of this action. Insertions must therefore be regarded as holistic units. While their holistic character is maintained, an elementary analysis is absolutely necessary. Consequently, we examined the inserted actions in an elementary analysis as well and compared their individual elements with the respective elements by which they were induced. The results were as follows:

132 insertions with all elements being similar	99.25%
1 insertion with dissimilar objects, otherwise similar	0.75%
Total 133	100.00%

We did not find a single insertion with completely heterogeneous elements, which does not mean that it could not occur in a larger collection of material. Such insertions may occur, but they are relatively rare.

Examples of completely identical insertions are those in which an erroneous action is inserted, because it was often habitually performed as an element of a series in the sequence of this series: I go into my room in the evening, and at the door I immediately reach out for the electric switch without noticing that the light is already turned on. Regarding the object, place and movement, the erroneously inserted action is completely identical with an habitual action which I have often carried out in the series "getting up from one's work on the veranda, passing through the door of the hall and the door of the room, opening the two doors, entering the room" the next element of which was turning on the light (No. 20). Such errors in turning the light on or off are habitually repeated by me in cases 30, 54, 133, 456, 648, 980, 1008, 1029 and by Anna in the cases 733, 759, 838, 1055. I am sitting at my desk, get up and put my hand to my nose to take off my glasses. The series 'sitting at the desk, getting up' induces the following element: 'reaching out for the glasses' which are hypothetically worn on one's nose. The erroneously inserted action is identical to the habitual one which is usually connected with the termination of writing or reading at one's desk. In this case, however, the test subject does not take into account that he has neither been reading nor writing at his desk and therefore wears no glasses. I take the watch out of my pocket and immediately press on the top of the watch. The inserted erroneous movement is due to the fact that many years ago I had a pocket watch, the face of which was covered with a cap. This cap was opened by pressing on the top, whereas the present watch does not have such a cap. By taking the watch out of the pocket, an action which is identical to that carried out years ago has been induced as the next movement. In this case it is obvious that parts of a series of actions which used to be carried out years ago can still have an effect after such a long time (No. 106).

J. opens the linen press at lunchtime and erroneously takes out his nightshirt as he is accustomed to do in the evening (No. 341). Further examples are case No. 419 where his vest is unbuttoned erroneously after his jacket has been taken off, although the vest is not to be unbuttoned and taken off in this case, and case No. 610 where the watch is habitually put into the pocket after the vest and jacket have been put on for an unexpected walk at night, during which a watch is the most superfluous thing etc.

Examples of similar insertions in which, instead of a habitual action, an action carried out immediately or shortly before with a partially identical object at the same place is repeated: J. throws a newspaper cutting, which has been lying on the desk, into the wastepaper basket and then erroneously throw a notebook, which has been lying on the desk beside the newspaper cutting, in the wastepaper basket too. The notebook and the newspaper cutting are both pieces of paper and thus partially identical, the place of action (from the desk into the wastepaper basket) is partially or completely identical, the throwing movement is identical (No. 859). J. is packing up books and then erroneously add a notebook to the books. The movement and the place of action are identical, the book and the notebook partially identical (No. 937). A. wants to change her socks, takes them off and then erroneously also pulls off her elastic stockings which are not to be taken off (Nos. 636, 637, 688). A. hangs various clothes in the wardrobe and then erroneously adds another item of clothing which should not be in the wardrobe at this time (Nos. 947, 948) etc.

Examples of cases in which objects are carried to a place correctly and then taken back erroneously. This type of insertion frequently occurs with Anna, but it does not occur with myself. A. has removed the blanket from the bed and immediately lays it back (No. 138, 828); correctly carries the fresh-made black coffee (No. 213) and another time a bowl (No. 249) into the pantry and takes them back erroneously; carries a towel into my room and then takes it back erroneously (No. 232); takes a tablecloth out of the cupboard when setting the table (No. 353), carries tableware from the kitchen to the table in the dining room (Nos. 930, 956) and takes these object back, etc. The object is identical, while the place and the movement show the partial identity of the opposite.

Examples of cases in which two objects are carried to a place correctly and then one of the objects is taken back correctly and the other one erroneously. These cases are related to the preceding type of insertions. Here the incorrect induction has two sources: first the transfer of the objects to another place, and secondly the fact that the erroneous return of one object is also induced by the necessary return of the other object: J. carried a glass of water in his left and a jug of water in his right hand, poured the water from the jug into the wash basin, and then took back the empty jug correctly and the glass of water, which should have remained on the wash stand, erroneously (No. 862). In this case, an identical object has correctly been taken to another place and erroneously been returned, while the sequence of places and the movements show a partial identity of the opposite. The other object, i.e., the jug which is returned correctly, is partially identical to the glass as a vessel filled with water, the place and movement of the action carried out with the glass and with the jug are identical.

Insertions that are anticipations. In these insertions, the similarity becomes an identity, since the inserted action is to be carried out later. There are 46 cases of this type in our collection, of which 45 are from J. and one from A. All these insertions relate to one and the same incident, namely going to the toilet in the yard which is also used by other persons. To avoid touching objects that may be unclean, such as the bolt and toilet lid, with their bare hands, the two subjects put on gloves prepared for this purpose. They put on these gloves in their apartment, and during 10 months there were 46 out of 1500 cases in which they erroneously took off the gloves immediately before touching the ominous object, namely the lid, which should not be done until the lid was lifted.

An insertion of an action with a dissimilar object showing similar characteristics regarding its position as a whole, while the place and movement are similar. A. takes (No. 921) various pieces of bed linen, sheets, blankets, quilts and pillows and lays them on the bed; then she takes a fur coat, which has also been lying on the table, and lays it also on the bed where it does not belong. The place (from the table onto the bed) and the movement (taking the object from the table to the bed) are identical.

Homogeneity of inserted actions and other actions carried out the same day. The inserted actions mostly show homogeneity with other actions of the same day. In the 46 cases where the two subjects erroneously took off their gloves, this action is not only identical to the one which should have been performed later, but also to several other instances where the gloves were taken off before and after the error on the same day, and homogeneity (partial identity of the opposite) exists with respect to the action of putting on such gloves, which is carried out several times a day. In case No. 419, where J., after taking off his jacket erroneously start to unbutton his vest, because this action usually follows upon taking off his jacket, the inserted erroneous action is not only identical to the action usually carried out after taking off the jacket, but also to the several instances where various items of clothing are unbuttoned or buttoned up the same day. In case No. 76, where J. gets up from his desk and erroneously reaches for his glasses to take them off, although he does not wear them at that moment, this grasp is not only identical to the one he usually carries out when getting up from the desk but also to any other instance of taking off his glasses in the daytime. There is also a partial identity of the opposite when he puts on his glasses.

The various attraction factors also include a type of attraction which can be perceived as an experience in the case of some insertions. The person concerned meets with an eye-catching object, e.g. an electrical switch which is then erroneously and unnecessarily reached for. This object induces the repetition of a habitual action, which does not mean that such an action cannot be conducted without this eye-catcher another time. Other objects virtually fall into one's hands, such as the notebook which is erroneously packed together with the books.

The separation of the ego from the task, where foreign objects, worries or pleasant thoughts concerning the family or financial affairs, things considered to be more interesting and more important than the mechanical implementation of the task or the purpose of the action, but not the mechanical implementation itself play a role, also has an effect in cases of insertions, as it has in substitutions and omissions.

We have identified heterogeneous and homogeneous components of insertions without assessing their effects and must now ask whether they are actually involved when an insertion is initiated and which role is played by each of them. The first striking fact would be that if insertions could be attributed to homogeneity, the result would not be omission but similarity support.

Let us now analyze our collection of insertions from this point of view.

The first homogeneity discussed refers to cases in which a series of actions which has already been performed earlier is repeated, with one part of the repeated action being an erroneous insertion. We shall later return to the law of the commenced and ended melody, on which these cases are based. The interlinked parts of the series attract one another in their predeterminative order. It is now to be asked whether, apart from the order-dependent attraction constituting an impetus in this case, the similar parts of the first, already completed, series attract the similar parts of the second series. In other words: if the series a b c d e has once been completed and a b c d is started for a second time, as a result of which e, although it should not be realized in this case, is inserted erroneously, does this mean that there is not only an impetus given from d to e, but also an attraction from the first e to the second e which is about to appear as well? If the e of the first series attracted the e of the second series, a similar inhibition should suppress the tendency for the second e to appear. Why does this second e appear as an erroneous insertion? If identity of the two e's could actually be a possibility, it should be supposed that the attractive impetus of the series has overcome the tendency towards similarity-based inhibition.

On the other hand, however, a similar inhibition must not necessarily develop when two similar units of psychological contents approach each other, and in most cases it does not occur. If it always occurred, no human being would be able to speak, write, read or to take a second step after a first one, because all consecutive two e's of a word would have to remain unspoken, unread and unwritten, and the first step would make the similar second step impossible. The inhibitions between the two e's can appear only if reading is not possible without restrictions, either because the exposition is too short or because the intention of the ego is split off or distracted from the performance of the task at this stage. With respect to the case discussed, we must therefore neither necessarily assume that a homogeneity-based attraction exists between the two e's of the series a b c d e and a, b, c, d, e, nor that the impetus of the commenced melody suppresses the homogeneous attraction and inhibition. However, it must be borne in mind that the erroneous insertion already indicates a separation of intention, which may lead to homogeneous inhibitions.

We are now going to analyze our second group of insertions where an object is first taken to a place correctly, but immediately after that is erroneously carried back to its former place, which constitutes an insertion. While the object in this case is identical, the places, because they appear in the opposite direction when the object is carried back, and for the same reason, the movements show the partial identity of the opposite. These cases are also subject to the law of the commenced sequence, although this happens in another form than that we have discussed earlier. They fall under this law because the first series of actions certainly induces the second series that would not be possible without the first one. In the case of a sequence, too, the ascending part entails the descending one, because no sequence can end abruptly after the 'ascending' part. It must not necessarily return to its exact point of origin, but at least to its vicinity[22].

Since the objects, places and movements in the insertions discussed are homogeneous in both directions, a homogeneous attraction and inhibition were more likely to develop in these cases, because their prerequisite, i. e. the separation of intention, was given. This problem cannot simply be dismissed by pointing out that a partial identity must not necessarily lead to

---

[22] The first ascending part of the melody of the Hungarian national anthem entails the second, descending part, that is to say, the second part is already given by the first one (Feuchtwangler, "Werkbewusstsein").

homogeneous-based inhibition. In this case, too, the attraction which the melody a b c d e has, owing to its reversal e d c b a, seems to be stronger than the attraction existing between the e of the first and the e of the second series.

In the next group of insertions, several subsequent actions are performed correctly with identical or partially identical objects, places and movements, e.g. two or three books are packed into a postal parcel. If a homogeneous inhibition occurred, one of the books would be omitted or a right book would be substituted by a wrong one. The above category of omissions is represented, for example, by the cases with 9 similar blankets and pillows. This, however, does not happen in the cases of the group examined by me now where a notebook is erroneously added to the books in the postal parcel, i.e. an insertion occurs. In the insertions of this group, too, the error is induced by the nature of the sequence. For example, three books can be referred to as a set a b c with a certain degree of cohesion and impetus in their order which cannot be stopped abruptly. Since the inhibition of similar parts is not obligatory, as has been explained above, we conclude that such an inhibition must neither occur between the two or three books themselves, nor between the books and the notebook, and that the sequence, when started, can overcome a homogeneous inhibition.

Now, however, two further questions arise: Why is a notebook, i.e. a partially identical object; erroneously added to the books and why not other objects lying on the same table and thus close to the hands and eyes, such as a pair of gloves, a cap, a ruler, a pair of scissors, a percussion hammer, an ear trumpet, a pen, a pencil, an ink pot and a vase with flowers? Secondly, if the separation of intention leads to an error in this group at all, why not to an omission? Any layman who is not acquainted with the science of errors will immediately regard the first question as absurd and say that the vase is so different from the books that such an error would be "ridiculous". This thought will occur to any layman, and we express it as follows: It is a notebook instead of, for example, the ink pot which is added to the books, because the notebook and the books are partially identical, whereas the ink pot is completely different. We therefore conclude that a similarity-based insertion occurred in this case.

But why an insertion and not an inhibition or a substitution? We have stated before that the homogeneous inhibition of partially identical elements is not obligatory, arguing, among other things, that reading, speaking, writing or going would not be possible if this homogenous inhibition were obligatory. We have also referred to the reading error in my study where a partially identical word in the next line had such an attractive effect that the eye of the reader jumped to this word and reading was continued without this second word being inhibited. I experienced a similar case in the form of a writing error when I was writing down this manuscript. When copying a passage from the first draft to the final version, I dictated to myself "der zwei e" (German for "of the two e"). I wrote "der zwe e" and thus left out the i of the word "zwei". Then a vague doubt arose: Have I written correctly? Consequently I noticed the mistake. Here the same thing happened as in the case of the reading error discussed above. That which concerned the eyes in the first case, now occurred in writing, despite the correct self-dictation[23], whereby the pen, due to the attraction exerted by the appearing identical element, missed out the next element, while no similar inhibition developed between the two e's. Since the letters i and e are partially identical elements in writing, the i is also suppressed by similar inhibition.

We have also explained that the separation of intention plays a more important part than homogeneous inhibition and that the former is the decisive factor for the occurrence of an error but not for the form of this error. In the above examples of reading and writing errors, one might assume that the intention returned just at that moment, after it had been separated immediately before. Thus only the first part of the Ranschburg phenomenon, i.e. similar attraction, which has been given relatively little attention in the literature up to now, occurred in these reading and writing errors, whereas the second part of the phenomenon could not develop, owing to the reawakening of intention. This hypothesis seems to be acceptable for the reading and writing errors presented, but it is not fully applicable to the type of insertions where the similar notebook, and not one of the dissimilar objects which were also lying on the desk, such as the ink pot or the vase, were packed together with the books. Here we must find another solution.

This could lead to the following idea: The sequence has been commenced in the form of book 1, book 2 and would be continued to book 3, book 4 etc., if there were more books lying on the desk. As a consequence of the commenced sequence, book 3 has developed psychological content in an anticipatory way. The psychological content involved a homogeneous inhibition, in which the partially identical components of the notebook and the book were amalgamated to form an integrated whole, and the partially different components were suppressed as usual. This would mean that two phenomena were involved: on the one hand the commenced sequence, namely book 1 and book 2, and on the other a substitution, whereby the commenced sequence would lead to an insertion of any kind while the substitution would be induced by the homogeneous inhibition.

Are these hypotheses true? If so, this would mean that, at least

---

[23] On the difference between writing errors based on correct and incorrect self-dictation, see my study published in *Arch f. Psychiat. u. Nervenkr.*

outwardly, homogeneous support played a part instead of homogeneous inhibition. In the case where the eyes of the reader, due to similarity-based attraction, jumped to the partially identical word in the next line, and this word was read instead of being inhibited despite its partial identity, the final outcome is homogeneous support. The same applies to the writing error discussed above where "zwe e" was written instead of "zwei e". In the insertion where the partially identical notebook was packed into the parcel with the books, the final outcome is support of the partially identical notebook as well.

We have stated reasons which could prevent a homogenous inhibition from appearing in these cases. These reasons are coexisting factors. The homogeneous inhibition would thus have been prevented by coexisting factors after the first part of the Ranschburg phenomenon, the homogenous attraction which entails support, has been completed. The homogenous support would thus be as follows: the first introductory part of the Ranschburg phenomenon would be realized, but the second prevented by external conditions.

Is there also a form of homogeneous support that is not only attributable to accompanying circumstances, which prevent the second part of the Ranschburg phenomenon? We now come to the question of practice, which exactly means that in the case of movements following one another immediately or after a time interval, the first movements do not inhibit but support the later ones, so that the later movements become faster, more skillful and stronger as long as no fatigue occurs. A collection of facts which is oriented towards the science of errors cannot include examples of such a form of support. In the case of practice, the homogeneity itself results in support, without involvement of the coexisting elements. Since the coexisting influences were only assumed as a hypothesis in the other cases, we must now, after dealing with the question of practice, also consider another hypothesis according to which this practice factor also plays a part in the erroneous insertion of the notebook into the parcel with the books.

The practice factor was also discovered by Ranschburg[24] in the process of memorizing, remembering and reproducing learned contents. He describes the amalgamation of identical parts as a summation, as an increased assertiveness of the amalgamated identical elements which can be identified in the phenomenon of practice. He adds, however, that necessarily there is also reason for a secondary inhibition as soon as the repeated identical parts or homogeneous elements following one another immediately (perservative elements) are to be understood or reproduced separately and independently. The interesting question concerning actions

---

[24] Ranschburg, Die Lese- und Schreibstörungen des Kindesalters. Marhold, Halle a. S. 1928, p. 193

in which the first steps do not only <u>not</u> inhibit but even support the subsequent ones, belongs to the field of increased assertiveness. A secondary inhibition does not occur here, which may be due to the fact that the intention is not only not separated from the task but is even present to a high extent.

In actions that have become automatic, such as going, the separation of intention exists, however, without causing a homogeneous inhibition. In this case, too, it may be the commenced melody which compensates for the tendencies towards inhibition. When we are running, for example, this commenced melody has such a dynamic force that it is impossible to stop immediately. This also applies to the act of running, and the manual activities comprising a series of elements, games and gymnastic exercises.

We have pointed out that the first part of the Ranschburg phenomenon, i.e. Homogeneous attraction, gets a supporting function, if the second part of the phenomenon does not appear for any reason.

I now must correct an error in my study on reading errors: On page 154, I discussed cases in which no homogenous attraction existed and, nevertheless, homogenous inhibition occurred. As an example of homogenous attraction and inhibition, I presented the case in which "dann" [then] was read instead of "Dieser dann" [This/He then], because the eyes were attracted by the second d and jumped from the first D to that second d. I also stated that in the case where "wir z. B." ["we, for example"] was read instead of "wir wissen z. B" ["we know, for example"], no homogeneous attraction was involved, because the eyes did not jump to the second w, but exactly that word was suppressed which began with the second w.

Today I consider this interpretation to be incorrect. The fact that the eyes jumped from the first w to a subsequent passage and left out the text in between constitutes a clear proof and a conscious experience of homogeneous attraction. In the opposite case, where the second word with the identical first letter is left out instead of the first word, we cannot find any proof of the statement that no attraction occurred between the two partially identical text segments. In this case, however, the conscious experience of attraction is markedly less. It is not clear why in one of these two cases the first word and in the other the second word is left out.

Such a dissociation of the two parts of the Ranschburg phenomenon is to be considered in various studies of this phenomenon, especially when dealing with the results of studies on response movements conducted by Ehrhardt, which are related to my studies, since they also concern actions.

Ehrhardt[25] tested the responsiveness of his subjects by means of a device which is used to test driving skills (Moede stand). The subjects were

---

[25] Ehrhardt, Neue psychol. Studien. 5 (1931), No. 3.

sitting in a car body and, depending on the requirements, had to turn the steering wheel right or left or to press one of the foot pedals or the brake when 5 red lamps, which were set up opposite and diagonally right and left to them, lit up. In the case of two-part series, i.e. when two lamps lit up one immediately after the other, the response time after the second, homogenous, stimulus was shorter than the average response time ,which was calculated on the basis of several thousand reactions. It is therefore not only to be asked here what kind of inhibition did occur, but also why the response was accelerated in this case.

In my opinion, this question is problematic, because the reduction or prolongation of response time is different from the inhibition, which appears as an omission or substitution in the reading errors, slips of the pen and tongue and errors of action. Here it becomes clear that the two phases of the Ranschburg phenomenon, namely homogeneous attraction and inhibition, must also be considered separately, since they may occur dissociated, which means that the attraction is not followed by an inhibition owing to circumstances discussed by us and perhaps also because of other circumstances that have not yet been clarified. In my opinion, the reduction of response times in the response tests conducted by Ehrhardt corresponds to the homogeneous attraction, i.e. the first part of the Ranschburg phenomenon. In the cases studied by Ehrhardt, it is a supporting factor which was not followed by the second component of the phenomenon. The reason why this second component did not appear in the form of an omission or substitution is another question requiring further research.

In my reading error, this increased speed of the response action might correspond to the fact that homogeneous attraction caused the eye to jump quickly from the slow and long way of following the line to the homogeneous point in the next line without leading to homogeneous inhibition. In the tests described by Ehrhardt, it might be assumed that the second identical stimulus was perceived more quickly than what happened on average, as in my case the second homogeneous word in the next line caught the eye more quickly than the text in the omitted line. Ehrhardt excluded any wrong reactions from his study which might have shown the occurrence of substitutions or omissions corresponding to the second component of the Ranschburg phenomenon. It would be desirable that Ehrhardt should resume the discarded thread of his important experiments and, turning his attention to substitutions and omissions, gather a larger collection of such errors to clarify whether, and in what percent of his cases, the homogeneous attraction was followed by inhibition in the form of an omission or substitution; and, if this did not happen, why the inhibition failed to occur.

It is also to be considered in this context whether the partially identical stimuli were received correctly or not. Did the test subject correctly see the lamps light up twice? Did he/she not confuse them? Did he/she react wrongly, despite having received the stimulus correctly? The question of correct or wrong stimulus reception may also be clarified without response actions, since the series "reception of the first stimulus, first response action, reception of the second similar stimulus, second similar response action", i.e. the interruption between the two acts of stimulus reception owing to the inserted response action, and the insertion of a stimulus between the two response actions, could be of particular importance to the final result. In Ehrhardt's experiments, where six different light stimuli and six response actions constituted a series of twelve elements, the problem is thus extended to include the question why the incubation time was prolonged in these six-element series (which actually were twelve-element series). A collection of substitutions and omissions had to be gathered for this twelve-element series as well, and each stimulus reception also had to be verified and checked for omissions and substitutions independent of any response action.

Gestalt factors, too, are to be examined from this point of view. If under normal conditions the test subjects make no mistakes, or only a negligible number, in these experiments, the study has to be extended to poorly gifted persons, or the talented subjects must be tested when they are tired, as we have to bear in mind that reading errors, slips of the pen and tongue, and errors of action do not necessarily occur with similar material and actually do not occur in most cases – we have already said that otherwise speaking, writing, reading, or any kind of action would not be possible. Instead, such errors presuppose that either the exposition was too short when the stimulus was received or that the acting person was distracted from the details of the mechanism by other thoughts or by the purpose of the action. For this reason, the errors in the exposition tests conducted by Ranschburg, in spite of similar material, did not occur in the first elements of the series, but in the last ones which, perhaps also for lack of time, are no longer considered with the same attention, and they disappear there as well once the attention has been drawn to these last elements.

In many experiments concerning reading and writing errors the subjects were directly tested in a tired state to provoke errors. The persons subjected to the Moede response test showed a completely different mental set, because they performed their task with a high degree of concentration. Ehrhardt concludes his study, which is particularly important from a Gestalt psychology point of view, with the following statement: "... identical experiences facilitate mental processing, different experiences make it more difficult." In my opinion, this facilitating by identical experiences corresponds to the first phase of the Ranschburg phenomenon, i.e. Homogeneous attraction, and the increased difficulty resulting from different experiences to heterogeneous rejection, which requires further research.

Now, the second question is to be answered. Why do apparently identical conditions lead to an omission of a partially identical element in one case and to an insertion in another case? In the preceding chapter we presented similar series of actions which induced omissions of similar elements, and in this chapter we discussed cases of similar series of actions which, by contrast, supported the erroneous insertion of a homogeneous but superfluous element. Why is one item omitted when nine similar blankets, linen cloths and pillows are arranged in a given order, whereas a similar notebook is inserted into the parcel with the books? Since both case are based on a commenced sequence in the same way, the difference cannot be attributed to the sequence itself.

It might be supposed that the long chain of 9 similar links is boring to the active person, who takes more interest in the remaining work of the day, i.e., that the mechanism is shortened to be finished earlier. The intention would thus be different in these two cases. In the case where the books are packed, the intention is split off from the implementation process, which means that the commenced sequence takes effect. In the case where the blankets are arranged in a given order, the intention is also split off from the implementation mechanism, but in addition there is a strong urge to accelerate the mechanism at any rate. Purely external conditions also have a certain influence. In the first example, the 9 items have been put in one place before. The acting person is prepared to take up all these objects, and upon finishing this series of actions he finds no other objects there. When he takes the last item, he notices that nothing has been left in the place. To insert another object, it would be necessary to get this object from another place, which would be a far greater error. If the books to be packed were arranged on the table in the same way as the items of bed linen were put together in their place, and if no additional homogeneous (or heterogeneous) object were lying on the table, an insertion of another element would be just as impossible as in the case with the 9 items of bed linen.

A further difference between the two cases lies in the fact that in one case a series consists of 9 actions and 7 items were first taken from another place and shaken out at the window before the series has been started. The 3 series thus have 23 parts with homogeneous objects and partially homogeneous places, while the packing of the books involves a series of only three separate actions. We thus have a gestalt-related difference as in the two- and six-element series in the study conducted by Ehrhardt. This difference does not seem to have a decisive effect, however, as is suggested by various examples, although they do not refer to insertions but to omissions. In these examples, omissions occurred in series of 2 elements, e.g. when the second of two door handles and the second of two bolts were omitted. In these short series, an insertion could not occur simply for external reasons, because there were no additional handles or bolts to make it possible.

In the case of insertions, too, the attraction was perceived by us as a conscious experience. Some inserted actions were carried out with objects that attracted the eyes or hands. The forms of heterogeneous distraction, where extraneous trains of thought, worries or pleasant thoughts concerning the family or financial affairs are involved, play a role in this chapter as well.

2. Mental Sets

When it comes to mental sets, too, it is often difficult to separate the perseverative from the anticipatory factor. Insofar as insertions are consequences of customarily repeated actions, not only perseveration but also anticipation must be taken into account, although perseveration plays a more important role. Where the original error leads to subsequent errors, as in the above-mentioned cases in which, for the sake of tidiness, gloves are mistakenly taken off just before they are needed, the anticipation of a later act dominates in the first case. In the repetition of the same mistake involving gloves, anticipation appears to play a more important role. It is, however, unclear whether the same errors which occurred beforehand did not have a perseverative effect.

Perseveration also plays an important role in insertions, in particular in the form I have described as the law of the commenced sequence. This applies to those insertions in which the erroneous action was once part of a series; it then reoccurs erroneously because the parts prior to it have occurred, i.e. the series has been struck up. I made 30 such erroneous insertions with several prior parts and 7 with one homogeneous prior part. Anna made 8 with several identical prior parts and 37 with one similar prior part. These makes a total of 82 out of 133 cases, or 61.65 % of all erroneous insertions. If we also include the 44 above-mentioned subsequent errors as such, 117 insertions in our collection, i.e. 94.76 %, can be considered a consequence of that type of perseveration which I refer to as the law of the commenced sequence. Even if we do not wish to attach an absolute value to this percentage, since we only have 133 cases at our disposal, it is nevertheless clear that the role of the commenced sequence is important for insertions; far more important than for omissions and substitutions.

The commenced sequence often corresponds to the frequency with which the series of actions prior to the sequence part inserted not only occurs in everyday life but also is completed after the sequence has been commenced. This is not, however, a rule.

Examples for the relationship of frequency to the commenced sequence in the case of insertions. If, in the evening, I walk from the veranda through the anteroom to my room and, upon entering my room, reach for the light switch in order to turn on the lights, although the lights are already on, the sequence with the erroneous insertion corresponds to frequency, since the lamp in this room usually is not on at this time; thus the person entering the room according to the previous series of actions must more often than not reach for the light switch (no. 20). If, however, during the day, I reach for the light switch when leaving the room in order to turn off the light which is not on, I am listening to the commenced sequence which induces turning off the light when leaving the room as a customary act in the evening; I perform, however, a rarer action since, when leaving the room, it is more often the case that I must leave the light on than turn it off and in particular during the day, this act does not have to be performed at all (no. 30). It seems that in this case the mental set has, in some indeterminate way, changed its focus to the evening.

When I take my pocket watch out of my pocket, hold it up to my eyes and press the winding crown in order to open the lid, although this watch, which I have had for many years and have, with the exception of a few years when I had a pocket watch with a cover over the face, which was released by pressing the winding crown, always carried with me; I had developed a rare and, for many years, unnecessary automatic movement. We could assume that in this case some reminder of the few years mentioned above led to this mistake. At the conscious level, however, I was not aware of such an association, but it may have been so fleeting that it escaped my self-observation (no. 106). - After using the small kitchen knife, but before placing it in the kitchen buffet drawer, I try to fold it together like a jackknife, which is impossible; this is also a rare action, since I seldom use the jackknife but use the small non-foldable kitchen knife almost every day (no. 291). The key to understanding this insertion is given by the fact that, after use, the knife is placed in the kitchen buffet drawer which contains a small, seldom used foldable knife which has the same size as the small kitchen knife. A momentary, and in this case identifiable, association helped a rarer sequence triumph. In some cases we cannot be sure whether the erroneous insertion has been activated by a more frequent or a rarer action.

In those cases in which Anna correctly brings an object to a certain place but incorrectly takes it immediately back, frequency and rarity seldom play a role, since such objects are carried just as frequently in one direction as in the other. Various influences intersect here, and sometimes a more recent action triumphs over a more frequent one, etc.

I was unable to find any evidence in my cases of the role of a feeling factor, i.e. that the inserted action was connected to desire, reluctance or a special interest or value. Thus we cannot say whether such a case could be found in a larger collection or not. The inserted action is always useless, if not detrimental. It would, of course, be easy to impute to the insertions a desire, a value or an interest, e.g. the attempt to open the non-existing cover of a pocket watch could be a case of thinking about a fond memory. I was, however, not conscious of such a motive and was unable subsequently to find anything similar. The affect and value problem can, however, as in the case of substitutions and omissions, play a role insofar as interest and desire turn to those problems which cause intention to be separated from the mechanism of the error.

The Hamiltonian principle of the least possible exertion of force does not come into play in insertions in the same form as it does in substitutions and omissions. When it came to substitutions, we were often able to identify a shortening of the purely mechanical performance, a short circuit as it were, although this shortcut not only did not correspond to the purpose but also contradicted it, since the erroneous action had to be corrected as soon as the disruption to intention was eliminated. The erroneous insertion does not shorten but rather lengthens the process. That which is simpler in cases of the commenced sequence is that less force is required to let the impetus continue than it is to stop it. Anticipatory insertions require more study with more material. Initial thoughts on this subject appear to point in this direction.

The separation of intention which, in substitutions, usually only applied to a small part of the action and only covered the entire course of the action in a few cases where the entire action was exchanged - in the latter it became active in choosing a different action - was cancelled in omissions for all elements of the action (object, place and movement). When it comes to insertions, this separation of the correct intention is also extended to all elements of the inserted action; it is, however, not passive as is the case with omissions but active as is the case with those substitutions which lead to an exchange of the entire action. This activeness is different from the above-mentioned substitutions since it is not stimulated from outside but instead reaches backwards or forwards in time and gains inertia in this direction.

It is difficult to say why insertions are less common than substitutions and omissions. We said that serious errors must be less common than minor ones, because they exert more resistance against error tendencies. Are the mechanics of insertions more difficult, or do external conditions give insertions less opportunity to occur?

When it comes to insertions, what is important is that they take absolutely no note of sensually striking phenomena of their environment. Not that the person committing the error does not register them. He does not eliminate them from his consciousness, but rather from his judgement. In this sense, too, the ego is split off from its environment. This is why, for example, daylight is ignored when a person mistakenly turns on the electric light; we cannot say that the person did not know it was daytime or that he believes it is nighttime. Likewise, we cannot assume that attempting to turn on a light in the evening when it is already on tells us that the person committing the error did not notice that the room was already lit. Knowledge about the time of day and noticing the light shed by a lamp have, however, run aground somewhere along the way between the sensation and the ego; this has happened neither before the peripheral organ nor before the center of these organs but instead along the ways leading from these centers to the highest psychological center of man to his ego. This, too, is a separation from the ego.

It is interesting to note the individual differences between the two test subjects, myself and Anna, when it comes to insertions. I, for example, did not commit a single error in which I took an object to a correct place only to mistakenly return it, while Anna committed a number of such errors. By contrast, Anna had only a single anticipatory insertion, while I committed these by the dozen. These differences indicate the necessity of investigating this matter with a larger number of test subjects.

JENÖ KOLLARITS

6 Repetitions

Of the 19 repetitions in my collection, 8 are from myself, 10 from Anna and one from subject M.A. Since repetitions are also insertions, they cannot be clearly separated from one another in many cases. While every repetition is an insertion, the opposite does not hold true, since not every insertion is a repetition but can, as we have seen, also be an anticipation.

The term repetition indicates that the error concerns all elements of the action - object, place and movement - should the error be carried out to its completion. We said that we consider even incomplete errors to be errors. When, for example, I take a book away from its place (no. 142) and then return to take it away again, this is a repetition, although I cannot take the book away a second time, since it is no longer to be found at this location. This is, however, impossible for external reasons only, whereas, for example, in case no. 175 when Anna takes potatoes out of the pantry and then mistakenly returns to again take out potatoes, the external circumstances make possible a repetition since the pantry contains potatoes in the same spot. If there were no potatoes, it would be impossible to complete this repetition. This comparison shows that it would be incorrect to separate these two types of errors from one another.

Examples of repetitions: When getting dressed in the morning, J. takes his pocket watch from the nightstand and puts it in his vest pocket, moves away from the nightstand in order to put on his jacket but returns before doing so to the stand in order to take the pocket watch and put it in his pocket (no. 64); J. takes off his glasses and then immediately reaches to his nose to remove them again (no. 973). - A. makes me tea, brings it to the veranda, places it on the table, makes me tea again, brings me a second cup, and only then realizes her error (no. 295); she washes grapes and then immediately washes them again (no. 432) and in one case washes her hands twice in a row (no. 534).

1. Attractions

Attraction factors can be found in all cases of repetitions, since the actions which lead to the error are repeated every day and often several times a day: the pocket watch is taken out of the pocket and put back several times each day, glasses are put on and taken off, fruit is washed, etc. All of these actions can have a perseverative or anticipatory effect on the repetition of the action. What is more, the first action has a perseverative effect, which leads us to an important point. The two actions which follow one another are similar.

Eye and hand attraction is also involved in all cases, since the person committing the error has the object in hand and in sight during the first correct action.

Differences are not suppressed in these repetitions, since the two actions are identical; in other words they do not contain different characteristics. Distraction is involved in the form of the separation of intention.

2. Mental Set Factors

Perseveration in the form of the commenced sequence is active as a mental set in all of the cases, since the first correct action induces the second, and incorrect, action. The everyday frequency of all these actions is, as we mentioned with the other errors, at once perseverative and anticipatory.

In my cases, I saw no evidence of the influence of value, interest and affect factors. Above all, it cannot be said that a repetition signals an interest or a desire or reluctance to perform the same action again; neither can we say that in particular those actions are repeated which are valuable or interesting or which emphasize desire or reluctance. If such emphases occur, they will likely appear only as an exception. By contrast, we must assume in all of these cases that time and effort have been lost, even if only to a minor extent.

As was the case with insertions, the Hamiltonian principle of the least possible exertion of force does not play a role here, since the action is doubled.

7 The Biological Value of Similarity Attraction and Dissimilarity Repulsion. The Klisis and Ekklisis of Monakov.

In describing homogeneous attraction, Ranschburg has pushed forward to physical matter and has noticed this attraction in electrical currents which disrupt one another as well as in magnetic fields, etc. He quotes the passage which I, too, have quoted in this paper from "The Tragedy of Man" by the Hungarian poet Madách on the attraction of related things and the repulsion of opposites, which is related to my 'suppression of differences', a theory for which I have fought without success for 20 years. P. Kammerer[26] has even spoken out in favor of the cosmic significance of similar things.

If psychology is a science in itself, then we cannot neglect its deep biological roots and must attempt to uncover the connection between the study of errors and, as Goethe once said, its "mothers." The best point of departure for such an investigation is the work of von Monakov.[27]

Monakov's work is based on the concept of the home. His home is the ur-Genesis, the continually igniting and latently glimmering "fire of life." As a result of the primitive instincts which spring from it, the *horme* secures individual as well as collective life into the most distant future. "This 'securing' of existence is biologically produced (in the nervous system) by the forming of "innervation alliances" (integration *a la* Sherrington) and alliances of energies: the association and merger of "physiophile" elements;

---

[26] P. Kramerer, *Das Gesetz der Serie.* 1919. Quoted by Ranschburg, *Az emberi elwe.* 1923 (Hungarian).

[27] Constantin von Monakov, "Gefühl, Gesittung und Gehrin," *Arbeiten Hirn-anat. Inol.* Zurich, 1916. - "Psychiatrie und Biologie," *Schweiz. Arch. f. Neur. u. Psychiat.* 4 (1919). "Versuch einer Biologie der Instinktwelt," Ibid. 8 and 10 (1921-1922). - "E. Bleulers Natur u. Seele. Eine kritische Besprechung," Ibid. 10 - "Die Syneidesis, das biologische Gewissen," Ibid. 25 (1934). - "Religion und Nervensystem," Ibid. 26 (1932). Summary and further work: von Monakov and Mourgue: *Introduction biologique à l'étude de la neurologie et de la psychopathologie.* Paris Alcan, 1928. Also available in German.

the latter I call *klisis* (affection, inclination, love). It stands for the temporary alliance of functional factors that promote the individual and collective prosperity of the creatures and at the same time for the expulsion of momentary damaging factors (physiophobe elements) or the crippling of their biological or physiological success: *ekklisis* (resistance, rejection)."

(It should not bother us that von Monakov sums up the entirety of human activity in one concept which he then divides into overlapping stages which range from the concept of the *horme*, a type of potential energy, to the primitive instincts, and from here to the higher instincts, to which he gives new names, since, according to his view, they no longer belong to the instincts. Von Monakov assumes the existence of five instincts: the formative instinct, which is responsible for tissue and organ development; the instinct to maintain life; the sexual instinct with its derivatives; the social and religious instinct; and, as a derivative, the *syneidesis* as a regulating principle in the event of conflicts between the instincts. This paper will not elaborate on this question.)

Von Monakov's view is in agreement with the attraction of similar entities and with the repulsion of different entities, since in the first case it is an "innervation alliance" to the point of assimilating the physiophobe elements which are the same as the physiophile elements, and it is a repulsion of the physiophobic elements, which are different from the physiophile elements. The assimilation of similar entities in Wundt, fusion in Binet, similarity attraction in Ranschburg, as well as my *suppression of different characteristics*, and the *attraction of similar entities* and the *repulsion of opposite entities* in Madach are given biological significance in the work of von Monakov.

The question we must now ask ourselves is how this biological significance comes into play in the study of errors. In answering this question we must first of all rule out those errors which are the consequence of external circumstances, in other words those which are not dependent on the person who committed the error. These include, for example, an observation time which is so short no person would be able to register the sensation, or externally imposed haste. Certain mechanical laws of the study of errors, however, remain in effect even in these cases. Those cases in which a person cannot complete a task as a result of his poor organization belong, from a biological perspective, to the indications of decline, and are of no further use once this insufficiency has been recognized.

If a healthy person makes one of those errors that are the focus of our work on errors of speaking, reading and writing, and on dyspraxia, this means, as we have already mentioned, that intention has been separated, often only from the performance of the mechanical work, and for short stretches; in other cases, intention has been separated from the action as a whole; it is not our intention to repeat this discussion at this point. This separation is caused by the fact, either that the ego is trying to solve other problems at the same time or that, if it has devoted its attention to the current problem, it is aiming at the final purpose and not at the mechanical performance required. The instinct of man or, in plainer language, his endeavor, is occupied with achieving the above-mentioned biological purposes, and these endeavors can be more important than, for example, laying nine different blankets and pillows on a bed, even if the person believes that this action must not be left unfinished.

Since the instinctual world gives preference to the biologically more important purposes, it must be during the performance of the mechanical action related to the task at hand that errors occur. Von Monakov would say that the person committing the error, is in these cases, was more occupied with the realization of innervation alliances, with *klisis* in biologically more important matters, than he is with the mechanical performance. In other cases, if the person committing the error is, for example, distracted from the momentary task by annoying events, he is occupied with *ekklisis*, i.e. with the repulsion of those dangers which are biologically more important than, for example, the blankets, sheets and pillows which belong on the bed or, for example, the ingredients which belong in a dish in order to make it savory. Von Monakov speaks of compromises which are made between various instincts or between two stages of the same instinct. The actions in which we are interested may also involve such compromises. When I write down this discussion, for example, I make a compromise when I devote my complete attention to the correct manner of writing each individual letter and do not allow myself to spin out other thoughts which in general would be more important than readable handwriting. It can happen, however, that an unclear thought arising from the mists of my mind will descend once more either temporarily or for good. If I chase after it, however, my handwriting will suffer.

A term introduced by von Monakov to describe the approach tendency as one of the two main behavioral vectors. See Ekklisis. (1972)

It follows from what has been said that not every error is an indication of decline or a disintegration. Decline, however, involves those errors whose origins lie in disorders of the nervous system or other organs such as glands (cretinism) which impair the work of the nervous system. The ailments mentioned at the beginning, e.g. fever, labored breathing, pulse rate, etc., are included here.

The indications of assimilation which take place with the elimination of intention in the lower levels of the relevant organs show that the attraction and assimilation of similar entities as well as the repulsion of different entities come into play in the mechanism of the action as well. This is a physiological and mechanical question.

JENÖ KOLLARITS

8 The Separation of Intention and Ranschburg's Distributive Inhibition

In his book about reading and writing disorders in childhood, Ranschburg speaks of a "narrowing of the so-called conscious field with respect to optical letter images and acoustomotoric sound images" and about a parallel "pathologically heightened quantitative distributive inhibition." "All the evidence points towards the fact," continues Ranschburg, "that it is the limited amount of oxygen available at any one time and supplied to the brain which distributes more or less unclear consciousness to the nervous processes in all parts of the brain which can be stimulated by impulses; by contrast, clear consciousness makes possible a small number of nervous elements (field of consciousness, perception collection, focus of attention). As we know, oxygen is bound to arterial blood, and we may safely assume that the quantity per time unit of arterial blood supplied to the brain during a waking state and in an affectless mindset is constant or variable within narrow limits. It is highly likely that, in the course of their ontogenetic development, living beings learn that it is in their best interests to concentrate their mental energies always in one certain direction only, which may change depending on circumstances. As we know from the studies performed by E. Weber, this is achieved - at least in human beings - by a special cerebral vasomotor center which, depending on demand, sends the required quantity of blood to the intensely working center by way of reflex regulation." According to this theory, distributive inhibition resulting from a lack of oxygen arises in the other regions.

In the relationship of distributive inhibition to the separation of intention, it is the separation of intention from the mechanical performance of the task, and in cases of substitution from the action as a whole, which is primary in healthy human beings. In the latter case, the first plan is dropped completely; in the former case, the ego is usually only separated from part of the action or from one of the actions in a series. This separation can be the consequence of distributive inhibition, as is likely particularly in those cases in which someone pursues two goals at the same time, e.g. mechanically continues to read or write while thinking of something else. As we know, the ego cannot sufficiently perform either of these tasks; under these circumstances we can read an entire page without having understood a word. What we can successfully carry out, however, are practiced automatic movements.

There are many different kinds of illness in this respect. The brain itself can be diseased and, as a result, unable to fulfill a task, as is the case with aphasia and apraxia. What is more, the cells of the respective areas of the brain can suffer losses in performance as a result of poisoning. In the case of labored breathing, the blood may contain insufficient amounts of oxygen to provide a proper supply for the working cells of the central nervous system and may contain too many carbonic acids, which act as a toxin. In addition, heart disease may lead to an insufficient amount of blood for the central nervous system.[28] Under these conditions, distributive inhibition occurs at a particularly fast pace. It would be interesting to transfer to apraxia the findings of psychological studies of dispraxia and furthermore to examine whether and to what extent distributive inhibition plays a role in insufficiently studied illnesses such as schizophrenia. The objective of such a study would be to see whether the person committing the error is unable at any time to read, write, speak or act properly, whether the error is committed only under certain conditions, whether at a different time and under different circumstances he can properly fulfill the task, and whether he fails to do so only when the task becomes complicated, e.g. involves longer series, etc. (See the work of von Monakov and von Goldstein.)

---

[28] S. E. Brack, "Encephalomalazien und Herz," *Arch. f. Psychiat.* 104 (1935-6) and the work of Lhermilte quoted in this source.

9 The Study of Error, Assimilation and Typology

"Tell me what errors you make, and I'll tell you who you are" (Kiessling) is something we will one day be able to say, once studies involving more material have better examined individual differences. Aside from remarks, little has been done in this direction. Such studies must cover a great number of test persons and several hundred cases of error for each one. Furthermore, it is necessary to avoid a sole reliance on experimental methods, which create more or less artificial and often unrealistic external conditions, but instead to draw from unbroken series which have been taken from the purposeful everyday activities of the test person. We know from the work of Jackson and von Monakov that a person suffering from apraxia or aphasia speaks and acts differently when he does so to satisfy his own instinctual needs than when he, for example, is to speak or carry out an action (e.g. salute) on command. The relative uncertainty of the typologies of such studies also stands in the way.

A study performed by Eta Hummers[29] interested us because it concerned assimilation, which is the basis for homogeneous inhibition, and because it examined the relationship of assimilation with experimental methods to the types proposed by E. R. Jaensch and Kretschmer. The author analyzed whether the integrated types of E. R. Jaensch could not (enlarge and) assimilate better than the non-integrated, as we would perhaps expect. She found, however, that there was little correlation between assimilation and integration and even less between assimilation and the types proposed by Kretschmer. We have thus arrived at a dead end and will remain there for the time being until studies directly devoted to error set us

---

[29] Eta Hummer, "Die Erscheinung der Verschmelzung und Vergrößerung, Steigerung und deren Beziehungen zu den Typen nach JAENSCH u. KRETSCHMER," *Arch. f. Psychol.* 95 (1936).

right.

Assimilation is, however, not only a phenomenon of the study of error, it is also a way of normal useful thinking, something which Alfred Binet[30] was the first to point out in his publications on "fusion," which have received little attention in Germany. The relationship of the assimilation of the study of error with normal assimilations, as well as the typological question for both areas of knowledge in relation to assimilations, lead us to a discussion of these problems. Without going into the details of Binet's work, which I have discussed in earlier publications, I would like to emphasize briefly what is necessary for our current reflections, namely that Binet discovered the role of assimilation in syllogism. It should be noted, however, that it is impossible for a syllogism to exist solely in and for itself.[31] The various parallel identical parts of the induction must have been assimilated before the proposito major of the syllogism could come into being. The line of thought was thus, with $+$ meaning "mortal," $A = +$; $A = B = +$; $A = B = C$ up to billions of $A = Z = +$.

This assimilation, which according to Binet is active as a fusion in syllogisms, and, as we have already shown, is contained in the induction necessarily preceding the proposito major of the syllogism, is of utmost importance for the typology of our perspective, since from this perspective there are two types, assimilating and non-assimilating, which play a role in human activities, in errors and all other actions alike. The non-assimilating types are the discerning types. The assimilating types perform synthetic work, the discerning types analytical work. Synthetic work is generalization, analytical work is differentiation, which is not to say that both talents cannot be united in the same person. Nevertheless, even in this case, one person is more synthetic, the other more analytical.

An example of the discerning, in other words, analytical, type was Jean Martin Charcot, the greatest neurologist of his time, who could brilliantly grasp the differences in similar phenomenon. He was able, for example, to differentiate the arthropathy of persons suffering from tabes from other joint diseases and to analyze dysbasia and paralysis, which until then had been treated together, and to find differences which had not been noticed by other researchers; differences which led to the discovery of amyotrophic lateral sclerosis. A synthetic achievement of the assimilating type was, by contrast, the work of Wilhelm Erb, who created order in the jungle of muscular atrophy by grasping the identities not considered by other authors

---

[30] Alfred Binet, "Fusion des sensations semblables," *Rev. phil.* 1880. *La psychologie du raisonnement*, Paris, alcan, 1911, 5th ed.

[31] A syllogism can only exist if an induction conclusion precedes it. The famous syllogism "All men are mortal; Socrates is a man; therefore Socrates is mortal" would in and of itself not be substantiated if the proposito major had not first been proven by the analogous conclusion "A has died; B. C. 8 people have died; all people have died so far; therefore every person is mortal."

and thus proving that dozens of diseases, in whose chaos scientists were at a complete loss, were one and the same illness.

Synthesis and analysis were united in the research of the Hungarian master of neurology, Ernst Jendrássik, whose synthetic, assimilating achievement was to unify inherited neurological diseases, despite their different outward forms; he did this by identifying common characteristics which other researchers did not notice. At the same time this was an analytical achievement, since certain forms, which were inserted in the framework of focus generation, had to be separated from outwardly homogeneous forms, for example, Friedreich's ataxia from tabes which until then had been treated as an associated disorder. A synthetic, assimilating achievement is his work on the basic principles of muscular movement in which, based on the 3 planes and the 6 directions of eye muscle movement, he came by analogy to the conclusion that these 3 planes and 6 directions are applicable to all parts (e.g. upper arm, lower arm, hand, finger, etc.) of the entire human body in which muscle organization is analogous to that of the eye muscles.

Mollier, by contrast, was not a synthetic, assimilating thinker, since he recognized this principle in the shoulder girdle muscles but was not moved to takes those further steps which Jendrássik took. In his work on trigeminal neuralgia, Jendrássik showed himself to be an analyst by finding differences despite outwardly similar symptoms, separating trigeminal neuralgia from neurasthenic facial pain and thus liberating many patients from useless and even damaging operations and from the extraction of large numbers of healthy teeth.

In his work on statesmen, Kornis[32] also examined these two types in detail and identified as analytical politicians those who steep themselves in the details of events, who differentiate between their ramifications and who also closely examine the thoughts of their opponents, whereas synthetic politicians do not lose themselves in details but instead "combine cases and attempt to subordinate them to comprehensive categories and principles."

"The primary work of analytical thinking is differentiation; it immediately sees where the cases differ and quickly detects the minor differences. The main characteristic of the synthetic thinker, by contrast, is the recognition of homogeneity; he immediately notices in what way various things are comparable and at once finds the most hidden homogeneity. The first is a shrewd politician, the second a thoughtful politician."

It is not surprising that Eta Hummer was unable to find a correlation between the assimilating type, which we also call the synthetic thinker, and the types both of E. R. Jaensch and Kretschmer, since, apart from mixed

---

[32] Gyula Kornis, *Az államférfi (The Statesman)*, 2, pp. 70 ff.

types, the assimilating and the differentiating types are likely to be found in both groups of the classifications of E. R. Jaensch and Kretschmer.[33]

---

[33] Some authors have wrongly criticized Kretschmer for having based his characters on pathological illnesses. His cyclothymia is in actual fact a normal type of character which only when aggravated turns into manic-depressive illness but has its roots in normal psychology. It does not correspond to a pathological or anatomical basis in the brain. On the other hand, he has been rightly criticized for his concept of schizothymia, which is derived from schizophrenia, an illness with an anatomical basis. My study of character (*Charakter und Nervosität*, Berlin, Springer, 1912) identifies two main types, one of which completely affects emotional life and whose aggravation leads to manic-depressive illness, whereas the other focuses more on the contents of thoughts and turns into its neurological correlate, i.e. hysteria, neurasthenia and paranoia, illnesses with no pathological or anatomical basis and which thus have no clear dividing line to normal life. Aside from Prinzhorn, no one has taken notice of this book, perhaps because it is before its time.

10 Practical Consequences

The importance of the study of errors for the prevention of mistakes is made clear by the case in which one of the simplest word errors, a partial identity of the opposite, leads to the sinking of a ship, when the captain confuses the words "right" and "left" in his order. In practice, the findings of the study of errors could be applied to the production of machines which have levers, wheels and handles which must be turned, pressed, pulled and pushed in different ways in order to start the mechanism. In order to prevent substitutions of these different objects, they should have different forms (handles), sizes and visible characteristics (colors, signs). In order to reduce substitutions of place, the handles or buttons should be installed far enough apart and on different levels (horizontal, vertical). Since two of the same movements (i.e. turning, pressing, pulling or pushing) inhibit the operator most easily, a turning movement should, for example, be followed by a lifting or pushing movement and not by another turning movement.

If Ehrhardt continues to pursue his experiments in this direction, practical conclusions could be drawn from his findings. Cockpit design, too, would benefit from such experiments. With respect to the practical consequences of the study of error, we would like to point out the work of P. von Schiller on Ranschburg's phenomenon and its influence on our ability to recognize automobile license plates.[34]

---

[34] *Psychol. technische Zeitschr.* 7 (1932) No. 2/3.

11 Summary

This study is concerned with errors (dyspraxias) committed by healthy persons and, based on a collection of 1100 cases, examined substitutions, omissions, insertions and repetitions on their own, and in comparison to errors of speech, reading and writing in other works by the same author. An analysis was conducted of the frequency of the various types of errors and the reasons for this frequency as well as the role of the Hamiltonian principle with respect to both this frequency and the various outward forms of the errors. This was followed by an examination of the separation of intention when errors occur and its variations in the various types of errors. This separation was also examined for differences which appear in schizophrenia, dreams and hypnagogic states. Furthermore, attractive factors were analyzed, *i.e.*, on the one hand Ranschburg's phenomenon in its two components, homogeneous attraction and homogeneous inhibition, and, on the other hand, distraction and the phenomenon which the author calls the "suppression of differences"; mental set factors were then analyzed, i.e. perseveration and anticipation, with perseveration including the author's "law of the commenced sequence", as well as the contest between factors active in errors. The analysis covered not only the elements of the action but also the action as a whole.

An examination was conducted of the biological basis of the phenomena studied and the parallels between Ranschburg's similar attraction which, if it does not lead to inhibition, can play a supportive role, and the *klisis* and *ekklisis* of von Monakov in the study of errors with their background in the world of instincts. The separation of intention was compared to Ranschburg's distributive inhibition. In addition, an attempt was made to grant assimilation, which is partially related to homogeneous inhibition, a typological significance outside the study of error; in this context the author referred to his work on character from the year 1912. Finally, as practical consequences of the study of error, proposals were made on how to prevent errors from occurring in machine operation.

(Received on 19 April 1937)

JENÖ KOLLARITS

After Kollarits

On the Nature of Human Error.

a.   General
        I have pointed out (Senders 1983) that most scientists of human performance have ignored error as a psychological/neurological process and have treated it only as an index of performance. In reality, errors are important behavioral events worthy of scientific investigation. This is particularly true given the demands of modern industry, where fewer and fewer people have control over greater and greater quantities of destructive materials and energy, and the consequences of error have grown accordingly. I concluded with the observation that "errors are what destroy us, yet all we have done is to count them and calculate probabilities. We know little about how errors are distributed in time, what form they have taken or will take, or what their real causes are."

b. What is an Error?
        The Concise Oxford Dictionary is relatively unhelpful. Error is defined as: "mistake; condition of erring in opinion;" mistake, in turn, is defined as: "misunderstanding of a thing's meaning; error, fault, in thought or action." Both appear to have some cognitive involvement implicit in them.
        It is useful to define error in terms of the underlying intention of the actor. Thus, if a proper intention is unfulfilled, an execution error may be said to have occurred. If the wrong intention was formed (analogous to the "erring in opinion"), the same action is now the result of a different kind of error: an "intention error." (Reason, 1977, calls these two kinds of error "slips" and "mistakes" respectively.)
        There have been many other definitions of 'error'. Swain and Guttman (1982) state that only errors that lead to important negative outcomes are worthy of attention. Adams (1982), correctly, in my view, argued that if human errors are to be used to define human reliability in the same way that machine failures define machine reliability, then all errors should be looked at, not only those that generate system failures. Sherican (1980) contended that errors should be described in terms of degree rather than all or none. I have difficulty in accepting that view, except, perhaps, in a situation where the intention itself might lack precision. Kollarits' collection or errors included only events that were either unequivocal

failures to do what was correctly intended (errors of substitution), the failure to intend to do anything at all (error of omission), or the intentional doing of what should not have been intended (errors of repetition and insertion).

c. Is Human Error Predictable?

At the micro level, errors may arise from random neural variations in the central nervous system and be quite unpredictable. Laboratory studies strongly support this position (Sellen and Senders, 1985).

It appears to be the case that the prediction of the next error is impossible. One can predict that error rates will increase or decrease if adequate data have been accumulated. Thus, it is easy to predict that the probability of writing 1984 on a check on New Year's Day, 1985, is high. One might have made the prediction, although slightly less confidently, even in the absence of data. Exactly when each of the 1984-1985 cheque-dating errors will occur cannot be predicted. The same limitation seems to apply to prediction of operator errors in nuclear power plants and the like.

d. Is Human Error Caused?

If one accepts the idea that an error is the consequence of an event in the central nervous system, then the error is caused even though we do not have a precise understanding of where and when the CNS causal event takes place. It appears simple in practical situations to identify the cause of an error by examining the sequence of the antecedent states of the environment and of the operator. Since error does not inexorably follow any defined antecedent state, it is probably better to accept the idea that errors are not caused by environmental factors or by psychological and physiological states, and that their probability of occurrence is influenced by the states of both the environment and the actor.

Models and Taxonomies

We can distinguish between these in the context of a system. A model is predictive: it is supposed to yield an output for any input, which is a good replica of the output of the system being modelled, given the same input. A taxonomy, on the other hand, is postdictive: it provides a limited set of names for an unlimited set of output events of the system.

a. Conceptual Models

Reason (1977) presents a model that is behavior-, rather than task-, oriented. The model contains information inputs and outputs, an intention system and store, and an action system and store. Reason focuses on how everyday errors are generated; he calls these "actions not as planned." His model is as follows:

1)   The intention system formulates the plans and initiates action to execute them and tests their progress. The simultaneous activation of more than one plan can, of course, lead to error.

2)   The action system is responsible for structuring well-practiced sequences of motor commands. It feeds back information to the intentional system about how the plan is progressing.

3)   Storage systems contain previous plans (in the intention store) and sets of actions (in the action store) to carry them out.

Other models with a similar structure were proposed by Norman (1981) and Senders (1983). Norman characterizes actions as the execution of schemata: organized sensori-motor units which control the flow of motor activity. Errors can occur in the formation of the intention, triggering of the schema and in the activation of the schema. Senders considers three sources of error production, which he calls intention, perception and action and further classifies the errors phenomenologically as being omissions, insertions, substitutions, or repetitions) following Kollarits (1937).

Kollarits' data show that about 70% of errors are substitution errors. At least some substitution errors may arise as a result of what Norman has called capture errors. Senders (1981) has proposed a quantitative theory of how such errors come about and states a number of experimental hypotheses derived from the theory. The scheme proposes that between each intention and its corresponding action there is a sequence of behavioral elements. He hypothesizes that the probability of a substitution error will increase as the number of common elements in two such sequences increases.

b) Taxonomies

General

Many taxonomies of error have been constructed. Some of these have classified errors as to their effect on the system being controlled. This attitude is the basis for the common tendency to report on and analyze only accidents and to deal only with those errors which were or were assumed to be the cause of the accidents. Other taxonomies classify errors according to the action that was performed incorrectly: e.g., the turning on of the wrong switch; and according to the circumstance under which the error occurred: in an aircraft or in a nuclear power plant. At a more general level, errors can be classified phenomenologically. We have seen that Kollarits used a four-fold system: substitution, omission, repetition, and insertion. The approach has the advantage of removing the error from the task-specific context and treating it as a generic behavioral phenomenon. At a more detailed level, errors may be classified as to the presumed cause or to the locus of the cause.

Taxonomies can be classed as behavior oriented, task oriented, or generic. The first type includes those described by Berliner and Altman in the 1960s, followed by Norman in the 1980s. The task-oriented type was typified by that of Rasmussen in 1981. Senders, at the same time followed Kollarits, and described a generic taxonomy.

In using a taxonomy to describe cognitive behavior in a situation where errors are the main interest, two approaches may be taken. One can argue that distinct types of errors or error mechanisms exist, such as omission, (Kollarits) or stereotype fixation, (Rasmussen), and the errors or error mechanisms themselves should be classified. The Rasmussen and Senders taxonomies are of this type. Another approach is to argue that since erroneous behavior is very close to correct behavior, structurally, spatially, organically, etc., the behavior leading to the error should be classified.

Behavior Oriented Taxonomies

The Berliner taxonomy is structured in a hierarchical fashion. The first level describes processes (perceptual, cognitive, motor and communication). The second level describes activities associated with the processes, (e.g. the identification of objects, actions and events is an activity associated with the perceptual process). The third level describes specific behaviors that occur during the activities, (e.g. interpolating, verifying or remembering during the activity of information processing). The fourth level gives definitions for each of the specific behaviors.

Altman developed a behavior-oriented taxonomy. His taxonomy is also set up in a hierarchical fashion like Berliner's. The first level describes behaviors as they increase in complexity: A) sensing, detecting, etc; B) rote sequencing; C) estimation with discrete or continuous responding; D) rule using and decision making; E) problem solving. At the next level possible modes of error are specified, e.g. the omitting of a procedural step.

Reason (1977) developed a taxonomy of the behavior leading to error by classifying 433 errors recorded in volunteers' diaries, according to the algorithm mentioned earlier. By noting where errors occurred, for example in the formation of the intention, he was able to classify 95% of them. Forty-one percent of the errors related to the forgetting of the plan or the preceding action and were classified as storage failures. Selection failures, the substitution of an inappropriate action sequence for the intended one, made up 37.2%, slightly more than half the rate Kollarits found.

Only Sellen (1990) usefully classified error detection (and correction) mechanisms. "Action-based detection" depends on "feedback from some aspect of the action itself, i.e. primarily visual, proprioceptive or auditory "Outcome-based detection" is based on the consequences (of the action) that "violates a person's expectations". A "Limiting function" causes detection "because constraints in the external world prevent further action."

Norman (1981) classifies errors as "mistakes" or "slips." "Mistakes" are errors of intention, whereas "slips" are errors in execution. Norman classified slips as occurring in the formation of the intention, the "activation of schemata" and the triggering of "active schemata".

Slips that occurred during the formation of an intention include errors in classifying the situation and errors resulting from ambiguous or incompletely specified intentions. The activation of a schema can be faulty in that it is unintentionally activated or that it loses its activation before it can be run off, so that an omission occurs. Unintentional activation can result from a capture slip--an old habit takes over inappropriately.

Slip-interaction with the external environment causes the slip. Slips resulting from faulty triggering include anticipation errors, where thoughts are confused with deeds and an act is omitted. Further, a feedback mechanism is postulated, which allows people to detect their errors. The mechanism includes feedback at different levels to monitor the many processes involved in carrying out an intention.

Task Oriented Taxonomy

Rasmussen (1981) describes a task-oriented taxonomy which is specifically directed toward the description of situation characteristics and analysis of events involving human error. The taxonomy was developed using categories of error derived from an analysis of 200 U.S. nuclear power plant "events" described by him (1980), as well as from knowledge of human information processing and performance-shaping factors.

Categories related to analysis of the event leading to human error describe the causes of human malfunction (e.g. excessive time demand), the mechanisms of human malfunction, (e.g. in the detection process), and the external mode of malfunction, (e.g. the commission of an erroneous act). The Rasmussen taxonomy does not separate purely cognitive from partially cognitive (perceptual, motor and communication) processes as does the Berliner, with the result that the "internal human malfunction" category contains some perceptual, some cognitive but no communication or motor behaviors. Some behaviors not included are important in error-producing situations. There is documented evidence of error having arisen during emergency procedures due to poor mental arithmetic and poor communication. Neither of these behaviors is included in any of the taxonomies.

A Generic Taxonomy

Senders, Moray, Smiley and Sellen (1986) classify errors by locus, by process, by mode and by expression. The locus of error is endogenous, that is, within the human; or exogenous, outside the human. If an operator incorrectly determines the system state on the basis of sufficient information, then the error would be endogenous. If a communication system is noisy, with a poor signal to noise ratio, even an optimal listener will make errors, and these errors would be exogenous. In general, endogenous errors call for retraining and exogenous errors for system redesign. (This gives rise to the sub-classification of error according to how to deal with it. In the endogenous case training, selection and luck are required; in the exogenous case, human factors engineering is called for.)

The next level of classification rests on identification of process. Errors may occur in perception, in intention, and in execution. The third level of this scheme is phenomenological: it describes the mode of error. The four modes are omission, substitution, insertion and repetition. Omission of a step may result from an error in perception or intention. Substitution may occur due to errors in perception, intention or execution; while repetition is an error in perception or execution but not intention. (Note that if there are errors in more than one step, correct behavior may result but the second order probabilities may be ignored.) Next, the expression of an error covers what was actually done and is strongly dependent on the task environment. Finally, the result of the expression is the consequence and is totally dependent on the task environment. The errors described by Kollarits demonstrate the reality of the notion that errors must be chosen from the possibilities (the 'affordances') that exist at the time.

Human Reliability

a. Introduction and General Background

The calculation of the reliability of a complex system like the medical practice of a modern hospital requires that a reliability be known or estimable for each component of that system. A system which includes human beings presents special difficulties. There are no widely accepted estimates of the reliability of a person in a wide variety of tasks.

In the context of reliability and quality control, human beings are troublesome components. They have failure rates that vary over an enormous range; there are great differences between people; the reliability of any one person varies in time and not in any simple way. Finally, unlike electronic and mechanical devices, people are self-healing. Human failure is a transient phenomenon. People who err usually recover and operate properly by the time the next task element is to be done; they may detect and correct their own error after, or, occasionally, before it has been expressed in the work environment.

Adams (1982) suggests that while the idea of human reliability is a sound one, methodological problems make it difficult to quantify. The physiological approach considers such factors as fatigue, motivation, intention and the like, that affect behavior in humans but not in machines. The remaining difficulty is that we do not know exactly what effect such factors have, since there are few data on error that do not cause a reportable event. The effect of fatigue, for example, might be to increase the error rate, but it might leave the rate unchanged and increase the size of the errors--how much they depart from what was intended.

To obtain adequate data on human reliability in a direct way one would have to run individual human subjects on a repetitive task for a long enough time for an adequate supply of errors to occur. Even assuming that one could persuade people to submit themselves to such a program, there is no guarantee that the results would be useful.

Meaningful probabilistic statements about human error can be made, as a rule, only under certain rather limiting conditions. For example, if the intensity of some signal is lowered to a value near the threshold, then the probability of detection will go down. The threshold itself is usually defined as that value of signal intensity which yields a 50% or 75% chance of detection. In most practical situations, however, signals are chosen to be sufficiently high, perhaps 100 times the threshold value, that the probability of failure of detection, if it can be estimated at all, can be inferred only by extrapolation from the lower levels of signal where measurement is easy. Direct measurement of very low probabilities is almost impossible, due to the large numbers of observations involved and the consequent changes in the psychological and physiological states of the subject.

In addition to problems of measurement and estimation, there are also problems of making generalizations, even about the person on whom measurements have been made, let alone about other people. Any person generates error data that are not stable in time. The statistics of error in complex situations may vary in both periodic and sporadic ways. Time of day (or night) is thought to create variation in a regular way. Time on the job causes complex changes. There will be learning (which tends to improve performance) and fatigue (which tends to degrade performance). Further, each person has his or her own ways of varying. For these reasons it is very difficult to deal with human reliability in the same way that we deal with machine reliability. However, there is a continuous effort to overcome the difficulties described here.

b. Two Approaches to Human Reliability

There are two general views of the human reliability problem. These may be labelled the Error Rate and the Causal Factor approaches. The Error Rate approach is very similar to that used in estimating the reliability of hardware components. As stated above, if a person were to perform the same task over and over until an error occurred and then repeat that experiment many times, one could estimate the mean time to failure and the probability of error per unit time. However, because people do not generate data which are stable in time, it is very difficult to obtain good statistics.

On the few occasions when error rates have been so measured, they cover a wide range. For example, in a simple task such as a well-defined sequence of control activities in response to signals, error probabilities between one-in-a-thousand events and one-in-ten-thousand events have been reported. If the errors are retrievable, i.e. if the actor becomes aware of the error about to be expressed and has time to alter the response, then the observed error rate is reduced by a factor of ten or one hundred.

It has been estimated that the probability of an error (including those that are changed before they are expressed) is between 0.2 and 0.02. Lastly, the probability that there will be a significant consequence of an error is the product of three probabilities: that an error occurs, that the error will go uncorrected, and that it will result in a serious outcome. For systems on which such estimates have been made, this works out to be somewhere between 6×10^{-5} and 4×10^{-7} per opportunity.

In vigilance tasks like those of a power plant monitor, error rates between 10^{-2} and 10^{-4} per opportunity have been found. The error was defined as the failure of the Human Operator (HO) to press a button within four seconds of receiving a combined visual and auditory alarm signal. The estimated range of the probability of making an error and failing to be aware of it is 2×10^{-3} to 2×10^{-7}.

Like hardware components, HOs can be connected in parallel, and what we find, of course, is that as the number of HOs operating independently in parallel on a task increases, the group performance goes up. That is to say, the probability that all members of a group will miss a given signal or fail to take corrective action diminishes with increasing N. Of course, when people are not independent of one another, there is less benefit from having more than one actor. The implication of this finding is that not all errors are related to external events. Some are internally generated; and the errors that are made by individual actors are not driven by a common process. The systematic decrease in error that is found implies that the errors are independent in time and magnitude. However, the solution may be impractical, except for vitally important functions.

The Causal Factor approach tends to ignore error rates or mean times to failure for human beings and attempts, via improved system design, to minimize error by consideration of external causal factors. This approach considers system design, documentation, training, environment and HO-machine interface factors.

c. Problems of Generalization

There are many data, and workers in the field have generated design prescriptions and proscriptions that should reduce the probability of error. Underlying the application of these techniques to the HO-machine interface is the notion that if a design characteristic reduces the probability of error in a laboratory situation, it will also reduce the probability of error when that design is incorporated into a larger system.

Similarly, the assumption is made that the results of studies of simplified tasks in the laboratory, in which the probability of error as a function of training can be shown to diminish almost to zero,will apply to human beings in an applied situation. It is probably the case that this latter is true. Training can always be used to improve performance, but it is a matter for cost and benefit analysis to decide how much training should be given before people assigned to a task are allowed to perform it. In the long run, unless it is necessary to make quantitative statements about human reliability or about the reliability of systems involving human beings, it is probably better merely to attempt to minimize error probability by adequate design, selection, training and motivation-- and hope for the best.

Some General Observations

Some of the introductory comments on the problems of dealing with human reliability bear repeating here: in the context of reliability engineering, HOs are troublesome components. They have failure rates that vary over an enormous range; there are great differences between HOs; the reliabilities of HOs vary in time and not in any simple way. Finally HOs may detect and correct their own failures after, or even before, they have occurred. The techniques used in estimating the reliability of machines are not likely to be appropriate to the analysis of the reliability of HOs.

Sheridan (1983) discusses the differences between machine error and human error to illustrate some of the difficulties in estimating human reliability. He makes the following points:

1)   There are many different theories that may be used to account for the cause of human error, unlike machine error that generally may be explained in terms of the laws of physics.

2)   There is no single agreed-upon taxonomy of error and hence data

collection may not be as objective as desired.

3)   People can recover their errors and so a true measure of human error rate is difficult to obtain.

4)   More than one operator is likely to be working at one time and the social interactions may affect human error rates in complex ways.

It is important to understand that, without exception, the methods described below rely on subjective estimation by experts of the underlying error probabilities. In every case the predictions can be only as good as the initial estimates. The few empirical data presently available are inadequate to support such estimates.

Some Reliability Estimation Methods

THERP (Technique for Human Error Rate Prediction) was developed by Sandia Laboratories (Swain and Guttmann, 1982). It makes use of an event-tree analysis of tasks, and its output is behaviorally oriented. Probabilities are used for events ranging from the incorrect reading of a meter, to a failure to perform high level procedural actions such as tripping a nuclear reactor. Performance Shaping Factors (PSFs) are used to modify the probabilities. These range from purely psychological factors such as fatigue, stress, set, expectation, time pressure, etc. to purely external features such as control room hardware (indicators, controls, and the like). The magnitude of the PSFs effect in some cases can be large, changing the probability of error by several orders of magnitude.

SLIM-MAUD (Success Likelihood Index Methodology-Multi Attribute Utility Decomposition) can, in principle, predict cognitive as well as behavioral errors. (Embrey et al, 1984). Its output is a probability of success and an estimate of its range. On the assumption that the logarithm of the probability of error is a linear function of Likelihood Index, estimates of error probability can be obtained by reference to two calibration tasks whose error probabilities are objectively known. It uses the estimates of subject matter experts as its input. It provides an apparently objective way to extract such estimates, but subjective estimates they remain.

OATS (Operator Action Trees) was developed at Nuclear Utility Services Corporation. This technique is based on an event tree approach, (Hall et al, 1982). Unlike similar event trees already developed for Probabilistic Risk Assessment, OATS specifically includes operator action, diagnosis and choice in the tree.

SHARP (Systematic Human Action Reliability Procedure; (Hanneman and Spurgin, 1984) is a method for performing Human Reliability Analyses (HRA) using the THERP and OAT models, and thus also depends on subject matter expert judgement for input. SHARP provides a framework for the use of these models within a systematic and regularized PRA. The framework is a logic tree that explicitly identifies and screens human error as a significant risk factor.

STAHR (Socio-Technical Assessment of Human Reliability) uses decision-analysis techniques and an influence diagram to incorporate some very complex variables into the prediction of error. (Phillips et al, 1983) For example the effects of morale, stress, teams vs. individuals, organization, etc. are added to the effects of the design of the control room, quality of Emergency Operating Procedures, etc.

SAINT (Systems Analysis of Integrated Networks of Tasks) was developed from a simulation of human operator behavior (Siegel and Wolf, 1967). The model is run as a Monte Carlo simulation to obtain distributions of errors, of completion times, of outcomes, etc.

EXHUME (An Exhaustive Model Of Human Error) was constructed by Senders and Moray. This model presents a way of distinguishing the causes and modes of error from their expressions and consequences. The causes and modes of error may be quite limited in number, whereas the expressions of error are essentially unlimited. The common emphasis on expression has made the investigation of error difficult and nonproductive in the past.

In all cases and at all levels of description and modelling, it is important to remember that errors arise within the actor. How they are in fact expressed to the outside world is a function of what the actor is trying to accomplish in the existing environment. The collection of operational data about modes will do little, data about expressions even less, and data about consequences nothing at all to inform us about underlying causal mechanisms. The model is a useful conceptual tool for thinking about human error.

Pierre-Louis Moreau de Maupertuis (1698-1759) is reported to have said to Frederick the Great that when there are many different cures for a disease it is most probably the case that none of them is effective. It is clear that none of the above analytic approaches satisfies the need for a quantification of human reliability.

There is a common tendency to blame the one to whom an error happens. Physicians, nurses and pharmacists may be criminally charged or sued in civil courts for damages consequent upon error. On the other hand, if errors are the result of random events in the central nervous system, blame is inappropriate. Kollarits' analysis of his error data was limited to the calculation of the frequency and percentage of occurrence of each type of error. He did not record the time of occurrence of each error, even as to morning, midday and evening. He had no basis for speculating about the probabilities of error or about whether they were random and unpredictable. Sellen and Senders (Sellen, 1983; Sellen and Senders, 1985) undertook experimental and theoretical investigations of the statistics of errors in a simple task. The results unequivocally support the randomness of the production of errors. The data also confirm the existence of both endogenous and exogenous random errors. Error should not induce blaming.

John W. Senders

Appendix One: The Statistics of Error

Many people blame the person to whom an error happens for any negative outcome consequent upon the error. But some serious investigators (e.g., D. Woods 2006) have chosen to abandon the use of the word 'blame'.

If errors are the result of random events in the central nervous system, blame is, indeed, inappropriate. Kollarits' analysis of his error data was limited to the calculation of the frequency and percentage of occurrence of each type of error. He did not record the time of occurrence of each error, even as to morning, midday and evening. He had no basis for speculating about the probabilities of error or about whether they were random and unpredictable.

Dr Abigail Sellen (see references) and the author have worked jointly on the predictability of error.

An understanding of the error generating processes in human beings seems to elude scrutiny—that of the unobservable error mechanisms. Earlier informal studies have shown that errors in a key-pressing task could be described as the result of a Poisson (mechanistic) process, and our model assumes that the internal activity that could lead to errors is stochastic in nature. Endogenous errors are those that arise solely as a result of internal factors. Our assumption is that such errors will always occur, with some probability, regardless of how well designed the environment is or of how well trained the operators are. Thus, at least some errors may be considered to be completely spontaneous in nature. The simplest way of modelling this class of errors is as a Poisson process, producing errors at a constant probability rate and therefore random in time.

If this model is a good one, we would expect the following hypotheses to be supported under ideal experimental circumstances: the number of errors per unit time will be distributed randomly, in accord with a Poisson Distribution. The intervals between errors will be distributed randomly, in accord with a Geometric Distribution. The autocorrelation of successive intervals between errors will fall to zero with a lag of one and will remain at zero for all higher lags; in other words there will be no periodicity of the intervals between errors. If a significant periodicity were discovered, an endogenous, time-dependent, error generating mechanism might exist, and one might be optimistic about being able to predict when errors will occur in time. There would be far-reaching implications for human reliability analysis. The probability of error will be uniform in time; learning, fatigue, and boredom will not be major factors affecting error rate in this task.

There are some logical requirements that arise in the design of any experiment aimed at internal error mechanisms. The first is to use, insofar as possible, stimuli that do not themselves induce error, such as an ambiguous display element, so that the observed errors will be spontaneous and internally generated.

A problem arises from the fact that error rates may be time dependent and related to the task. The subject may exhibit learning effects on the one hand and fatigue and boredom on the other, and these may result in changes in error rate during the performance of the task. If such factors were tied to the error generating process, one would expect to see a non-uniform distribution of errors over time.

Errors in our experiment were defined in the context of the task as either an incorrect keypress or as a failure to make a response within a time limit. The brief time allowed for a response illustrates one of the major drawbacks in conducting research on human error: detectable errors usually occur so infrequently that it is impractical to obtain a large enough sample to make valid estimates of their probability or their distribution in time. Imposing a time limit has at least two effects. One of these is to make the task more difficult and the second is to reduce the time available for the self-detection and correction of errors. Not only does the number of errors in a sample of behavior increase, but the observed error rate is closer to the true error rate in the absence of the opportunity to self-correct. The major disadvantage of the imposition of time limits to induce error production is that we cannot be sure that the mechanisms are the same as those that function under non-stressed conditions.

Eight subjects observed 100 different sequences of three digits (0-9) stimuli. In one half of the stimuli, requiring a Q response, the first digit was the smallest and the third was the largest.

In the other half, requiring a P response, the first digit was the largest and the second was the smallest. Each subject was instructed to respond on every presentation of a stimulus that could last up to 1 second. After a response, or the passage of 1 second, the stimulus was replaced by the next stimulus. The task was therefore predominantly subject-paced.

The 100 stimulus items were selected randomly, without replacement, for each of 10 sets. There were 1000 presentations to each subject.

Results

The data set for each subject was divided into 20 intervals of 50 trials each. For every subject, we could not reject at the .05 level the hypothesis that the distribution of number of errors per group of 50 is Poisson.

The lengths of the intervals between errors--both incorrect keypresses and failures to respond--were tabulated. For 7 of the 8 subjects, we could not reject at the .05 level the hypothesis that the distribution of intervals between errors is Geometric. The tests for goodness of fit of the Poisson and Geometric distributions do not preclude the possibility that there may be an underlying periodicity in the data. We examined this possibility by computing autocorrelations of the intervals between errors over the range 1 through 20 without wraparound. Only four of the 160 correlations were found to be significant at the .05 significance level. There is no reason to believe that these are not due to chance, since we might expect 8 (5% of the 160) correlations to be significant under the null hypothesis.

We summed the numbers of errors made by all subjects for each of the 100 different stimulus items and tested the uniformity of the distribution of errors over items. The null hypothesis that the expected number of errors per item was constant was rejected,(Chi Sq (99) = 489), p < .001. Close inspection of items with unusually high error rates revealed that they were of a special form. Items requiring a Q key press were more likely to be those that began with a low digit. Items requiring a P key press were more likely to be those that began with a high digit. It was clear that some subjects sometimes made a decision based on the first digit of the sequence rather than processing all three. When this occurred, items not conforming to the expectation tended to elicit more errors. For example, the overall probability of error per item averaged over all eight subjects was .061; however, of the 80 occasions that the stimulus "7 8 9" was presented, 33 of the responses were in error. For 90 of the 100 items we cannot reject the hypothesis that the obtained results are drawn from a binomial distribution (Chi Sq (7) = 9, p > .05). The remaining 10 items were deviant from expectation.

The complete set of data for each subject was subdivided into 20 equal intervals of 50 trials each. Each interval, then, represented half of one set of 100 stimuli. The total number of errors made by all subjects within an interval was summated.

For all subjects we could not reject the hypothesis of a constant error rate across time (Chi Sq (19) = 29, p > .05). Errors were not significantly dependent on test-item position throughout the experimental session.

Discussion

We believe that there are two error-generating mechanisms: one is responsible for endogenous errors; the other for exogenous ones. The data support the simple view that most of the errors that occurred in this experiment were the output of an endogenous random error generator. Some small portion of the errors in this task are attributable to the specific properties of the stimuli themselves. These item-related errors are exogenous: tied to external factors.

Much may be learned from an examination of the distributions of error distributions. The foregoing analysis appears to show that errors occur in accord with well-established rules governing the behavior of random events. Therefore the time-course of erroneous behavior cannot be predicted. A model consistent with these results is that errors are generated by random internal processes. In brief, if a hypothetical lump of 'erronium' in the brain emits an 'erron' when you are about to do something, you blow it!

John. W. Senders

Appendix Two: Death in the Errogenous Zone

There continues to be hospital deaths due to human error.

Inquests and courts convene to look at what people have done and frequently find that the hospital death was the result of an error. Then they blame someone for the death. Is that right and just? Or is it the continued need to blame someone for every bad outcome? The newspapers carry stories of medical misadventure. The public becomes justifiably alarmed.

I have attempted to alter this state of affairs. My avowed purpose has been to make psychologists think about errors as psychological events worthy of investigation in their own name. As I stated in the Introduction, in 1980, with the collaboration of Ann Crichton-Harris, my office organized and supported an international conference on the nature and source of human error, the first of its kind to our knowledge. We found many people interested, but only two beside myself who were actually working on the problem. It was a successful meeting, and we believe it made many people think about error as the object of study and not only its effect. The second conference on error was held in1983 under more affluent sponsorship than the first could provide: NATO and the Rockefeller Foundation.

Definitions

The study of error is inextricably mixed with the study of accidents. Accidents are not psychological events. They are mostly physical events. Not all accidents are the result of error, nor do all errors lead to accidents. This latter is most fortunate, since, if all errors did result in accidents, the accident rate in all forms of aviation, for example, would be much greater.

It is tempting to consider error as a difference between intention and action. Thus, if I approach a traffic light which is red, see it as red, correctly decide to stop but accelerate instead, I have made an error in the execution of my intention. I shall call this an execution error.

I might have seen the light as red, decided to go through it and executed that decision correctly. This error is a difference between what should have been intended and what was intended. This is an intention error.

I might have misperceived the light as green, properly decided to go through it and correctly executed the intention. This would be a perceptual error.

This classification scheme is based on some presumed process inside the person.

Other errors arise from processes, events and states outside the erring person: the exogenous errors. We tend to think of training as reducing the former, endogenous errors, and 'human factors engineering' as reducing the exogenous ones

Another classification arises from the nature of the errors. Everyone is familiar with errors of omission. If one does not do what should have been done, there has been an error of omission. If one does something again that has already been done, then there has been an error of repetition. If one does something when nothing should have been done, there has been an error of insertion. Finally, if one does the wrong thing, executes the wrong action, or acts in the wrong place or at the wrong time, an error of substitution has occurred.   This latter is a broad category. Kollarits' data show that nearly 70% of the errors he recorded were substitution errors. This class may be the most fruitful to investigate.

If we go back to the example of the red light, it was probably a substitution error of an endogenous nature. We are uncertain about the process involved. It could have been exogenous, a problem with the light, but until we have studied the traffic light and the circumstances, we cannot tell.

Some Queries

Are errors caused? Freud thought so, but I believe that just as "sometimes a cigar is just a cigar", so sometimes an error is just an error. Some errors in aviation may be Freudian slips; probably most are not.

To say that a behavioural event is not caused is likely to arouse anxiety in the minds of most psychologists. Yet it may very well be that errors are like quantum mechanical events, which have probabilities of occurrence but are not considered to be caused in any particular instance. If errors are without cause, they partake of the flavor of Acts of God in law, and it may very well be the case that one should not be responsible for such 'mental' Acts of God. The implications for legal responsibility are disturbing. One can easily imagine the difficulties that a psychologist expert witness would face in court in attempting to establish responsibility in the face of the apparent causelessness of error.

If errors are due to the central nervous system, we should be able to detect the difference in state before an error and the state before a correct act, and predict the error. This raises another question.

Can the time of errors be predicted? Experimental data on the statistics of error are rare. Very few experimenters collect data on when errors occur so that the statistics of inter-error intervals an be computed. My own findings indicate that the distribution of inter-error intervals, in terms of the number of opportunities for error, is exponential to a good level of fit. Not only is the chi-square less than the critical value, it is also the case, and one should always be alert for such things, that the mean and the standard deviation of the distribution, for one subject at a time, are almost identical. Similarly, the number of errors per unit block of opportunities is a very good fit to a Poisson distribution where the mean and the variance of the number are almost identical. Of course, if errors were caused by some constant probability event, then we might be able to detect the event and predict the error. This is an unlikely discovery.

Can the form of an error be predicted? Here one can be more hopeful. Errors of action are not chosen at random from the domain of all possible actions. Actions done in error are, for the most part, psychologically or physically, or both, near the things that should have been done. If one intended to raise the flaps after take-off, it is unthinkable that one would instead open a window. It is more likely that one would overlook the raising of the flaps--an error of omission--or actuate an adjacent control--a substitution error.

It is possible to present an elementary model of how one might predict what kinds of errors are likely to be made and how one might analyze and redesign to minimize or eliminate them.

Would it be desirable to eliminate human error? Although there may be some circumstances in which there would be unanimous approval of this goal, there are some others where it seems better to tolerate the errors. I suspect that errors are the reverse of the coin of creativity. That a person completely without error would be lacking in invention and creativity and would also be a dull companion. I suspect that creative people make more errors than the less creative. I know of no data that support this hunch and leave it to others to explore.

A Model of Error Production

Kollarits recorded errors he made, a few made by his wife and his colleagues and concluded that most errors in everyday life were substitution errors. A typical substitution error would be: "I dip my pen into my coffee cup instead of into the inkwell which stands next to it." Personally, on occasion, I have poured, or started to pour, wine into my coffee cup instead of into my wineglass that stands next to it. The coffee cup errors are not the result of a poor aim. They are precisely programmed departures from the correct action. Had they been aiming errors, more often the wine would end up on the tablecloth than in the coffee cup. The wrong destination is programmed in some way and carried out flawlessly, unless the original intention intervenes. When one is pouring wine, one does not pour it over one's shoulder onto the floor. That can be predicted with confidence.

Like the psychologist, William James, I have started to change my shoes and found myself undressed and in bed without any knowledge of why I am there. This error has been reported by many other people. This error has been reported by many other people. It suggests that the two processes are closely related and that one got substituted for the other. The model of error production covers both types.

Consider the drawing below in Figure 1. There is a domain of intentions on the left and a domain of actions on the right. Between are successive elements which enter into the process which intervenes between intention and execution. Although it is easier to visualize these elements as being external to the human being, like things to be done in the cockpit or workplace, they can equally well be stages in information processing or retrieval.

Figure 1. A model of error production.

Domain of Intentions				Domain of Actions		
A	*	*	o*	o*	*	*a
B	o	o	o	o	o	b
C	*	*	*	*	*	*c

Intention A is supposed to result in action a; intention B in action b. The intervening stages have some elements in common. The number X is the measure of the number of common elements in uninterrupted sequence. X quantifies the commonality of the processes intervening between A and a and B and b.

The paths for actions a and b diverge from the last common element at some distance from the domain of actions. The number Y is the measure of that distance and is the number of elements or stages between the last common element and the actions. Lastly, it is assumed that behaviour will be trajectory-controlled to a greater or lesser degree. It is not only where you are, but also how you got there, that determines the probabilities of where you go next. The number W is the measure of the 'length' of trajectory control in terms of number of elements or stages.

It is possible to construct a synthetic task or to analyze real world tasks with precise values of X, Y and W. Here are some hypotheses:

1. As X increases, the probability of substitution of a for b (and v.v.) increases monotonically.
2. As Y increases, the probability of substitution of a for b (and v.v.) decreases monotonically.

3. As W increases, the probability of substitution of a for b (and v.v.) decreases monotonically.
4. For any value of W it will be possible to increase X so as to cause a sudden increase in probability of substitution of a for b (and v.v.).
5. The interpolation of redundant or meaningless stages or elements between the point of divergence and the domain of action will decrease the probability of substitution of a for b (and v.v.).

Most of these hypotheses are in accord with intuition. In fact, designers commonly use a 'guard' over critical switches. I suspect that the guard is intended more to allow intention to overcome an incorrect reaching for the guarded switch as a result of a low level of W than as a protection against inadvertent operation of the switch with, say, the shirt sleeve. It is reaching for the wrong switch that is guarded against.

Task Analysis can reveal which tasks have much in common (large X) and which have little (low X). W can be controlled by training, motivation (whatever that may be) and by avoidance of fatigue. The measurement of W can be achieved by manipulating X, as in hypothesis 4. That would be a fruitful place to start on a research program.

Many other experiments can be conceived which derive from this simple model of error generation.

There are many design decisions that are worth doing at the outset if one wishes to reduce the probability of certain errors or perhaps to eliminate them. In general, if you wish to make sure that b is not done when a is intended, place the control for b as far away from the control for a as possible; provide highly redundant identification of b as b: introduce unnecessary steps in the terminal sequence of elements which lead to b; introduce unnecessary steps in the sequences in which X (commonality) is large; keep the performance under the control of intention by avoiding the automation of behaviour and thereby keeping W (memory of intention) as large as possible. This last is most important: intention must be maintained in control if self-detection of error is to occur.

Conclusion

It is time that psychologists begin to study error differently. In Aviation Psychology we have concentrated too much on correct behaviour. It is the errors that destroy us, yet all we have done is to count them and calculate probabilities. We know little about how often errors occur and virtually nothing about what the errors are or will be. Today, fewer and fewer people are in control of more and more energy, toxic material and human lives. The consequences of error have grown accordingly. In earlier times a worker who made a serious error was likely to injure or kill himself.

Today a transportation error, an industrial error, or a political error can kill hundreds, waste billions, or, and fortunately it has not yet happened, start a war that could destroy the planet.

John W. Senders

Appendix Three: Theory and Analysis of Typical Errors in a Medical Setting

Introduction

First things first: 'medical error' is not 'medicine', it is 'error.' The discipline appropriate to its study and diagnosis is not medicine but theory of error -- errororology! What is involved is a part of the study of human behavior. That errors happen to occur in a medical setting is the reason for my speaking here. If the identical error happened to occur in a nuclear power plant, I would be saying very similar things to a meeting of nuclear power specialists, with some variation in nomenclature, of course.

It has been repeatedly said, over thousands of years, that to err is part of being human. For example:

Errare Humanum Est: to err is human. (Probably a variation on Plutarch, Morals, c 100 AD)

"I presume you're mortal, and may err." (Shirley, The Lady of Pleasure, 1635)

"To err is human; to forgive divine." (Pope, Essay on Criticism 1711)

"To err is human; to forgive is against company policy." (Senders, various, 1978)

All of these quotations state that errors will be made by people despite their determination to avoid them. Yet people are consistently held accountable for their errors when they lead to accidents and adverse outcomes. Is this proper? I argue that it is not, in the same way that in law no-one is held accountable for acts of God.

The Distinction Between Errors and Accidents

What is an error? From the external viewpoint, an error is a failure to perform an intended action that was correct given the circumstances. In my view an error can occur only if there was or should have been an appropriate intention to act on the basis of a perceived or a remembered state of events; and if the action finally taken was not that which was or should have been intended.

An error is not defined by an adverse or serious outcome. An adverse outcome may occur with no error, if the intention was the proper one, the action was properly executed, and the outcome was probabilistic in nature--as in playing a game, in deciding whether to carry an umbrella, or in performing an operation known to be risky.

What is an accident? An accident is an unplanned, unexpected, and undesired event, usually with an adverse outcome. An adverse outcome after an error, by this definition, must be construed to be an accident. No one plans an error; no one expects an error; no one desires an error.

The Relation Between Errors and Accidents

An error is a psychological event with psychological causes, if errors are caused at all. There is always the possibility that causes of all or some errors cannot be identified. An error may have any of a possibly large number of causes. A defined causal mechanism can give rise to a taxonomy of errors. There are many possibly causal taxonomies of error.

Some Taxonomies of Error

Internal Processes, Input Error or Misperception: the input data are incorrectly perceived, an incorrect intention is formed, and the wrong action is performed; that is, an action other than what would have been intended had the input been correctly perceived. For example, I may be confronted by the phrase "1000 mg" and see it as "100.0 mg". I decide that it should be administered as a bolus into a Y-port and I successfully do so. A fatal overdose results.

Intention Error or Mistake: the input data are correctly perceived, an incorrect intention is formed, and the wrong action is performed; that is, an action other than what should have been intended, given that the input was correctly perceived. For example, I may be confronted by the phrase "1000 mg" and see it as "1000 mg". I incorrectly decide that it should be administered as a bolus into a Y-port and I successfully do so. A fatal overdose results.

Execution Error or Slip: the input data are correctly perceived, the correct intention is formed, and the wrong action is performed; that is, an action not what was intended. For example, I may be confronted by the phrase "1000 mg" and see it as "1000 mg". I correctly decide that it should be administered as a drip after dilution in a drip bag. I become distracted while approaching the patient and, from habit, inject the contents as a bolus into a Y-port. A fatal overdose results.

Attribution to Locations: Endogenous Error is an error which arises from processes inside the instigator. The elimination or reduction of such errors must involve psychology, physiology or neurology. The error resulting from distraction cited above is 'endogenous.' It probably results from the capture of a lower probability process-- injection into a bag-- by a higher probability process--injection into a Y-port--the two processes sharing common elements of action.

Exogenous Error is an error which arises from processes outside the instigator. The elimination or reduction of such errors must involve engineering and design of objects and work environments. The error may arise from the occasional use of extraneous ".0" since this allows the false interpretation of "2000" as "200.0". Better yet, the error could be reduced in probability by the spelling out of the amount as "Two Thousand" since this will rarely, if ever, be read as "Two Hundred".

Mode

If an error results in an action, then there is a phenomenon which can be observed. This we may call its "mode". One reasonable taxonomy of error modes is:

Error of Omission: an error characterized by the leaving out of an appropriate step in a process.

Error of Insertion: an error characterized by the adding of an inappropriate step to a process.

Error of Repetition: an error characterized by the inappropriate adding of a step normally appropriate to a process.

Error of Substitution: an error characterized by an inappropriate object, action, place or time, instead of the appropriate object, action, place or time. This may be an omission of a step followed by an insertion of some other, inappropriate, step.

How to Talk About Errors

It is common to discuss errors in medical settings in terms of their expressions, what was done wrong, or in terms of their consequences, what happened to the patient. We see, as a rule, only those consequences that result in injury or death. The number of errors involving Lidocaine, for example, is an interesting statistic, but it does not tell us much about why the errors occurred. What we don't see are those errors that occurred and were caught before they were completed. We do not have an estimate of the probability of substitution errors on the night shift, or by physicians, or by pharmacists. The mode of an error is a datum of great importance. It could help us in estimating the risk of the introduction of a new drug, a new package, or a new device into the hospital.

As we have seen the mode of an error is its expression, i.e., something wrong done in a particular environment. The expression must depend on what is available to be done. In a medical setting, an error of substitution may result in a nurse's picking up a 2 gram prefilled Lidocaine syringe (its expression) instead of a 100 mg syringe. In a nuclear power plant the same error might be expressed by turning off the wrong pump. The error is the same in both cases: a wrong act has been substituted for the right act.

Finally there is a consequence--what happens as a result of what was erroneously done. That is, the accident caused by the error. The syringe substitution error can result in a massive overdose of Lidocaine.

What Can Be Done About Errors?

An error can occur, can be detected and even corrected at points in the sequence of *mental* events between perception and the resulting action. An error can occur, and can be detected and corrected at points in the sequence of *physical* events between the beginning and the end of an action. Error detection can be of the error's mode, of its expression, or of its consequence. For example, a nurse may start to reach for a 2 gram Lidocaine syringe and change the motion towards its correct goal, the 100 mg syringe. This correction might be a conscious act or not; little has been done on the analysis of incipient errors. A nurse may actually pick up the wrong syringe and replace it with the correct one, and so on. There are many opportunities for detection. Personal experience tells us that the probability of such self-corrected errors will be high, and that such errors are common. Data gathered by Senders and Cohen suggest that for every error completed by nurses (e.g., the actual use of a wrong syringe) there are about ten which were caught before they actually were completed, so that there was no accident and, therefore, no report. Errors are much more common than we might like to think.

For the internal points in the sequence, the mental events, possible remedial actions must be psychological in nature. Sellen has suggested the possibility of training in the use of tactics leading to improved probability of self-detection of error. For the external points in the sequence there must be systems analysis and redesign of elements of the system and the system as a whole. The goal of such redesign: of means of use, of packaging, of labeling, of warnings, is to make the object announce its identity to the user through many independent and redundant routes.(6) In an ideal world, a prescription would say in clear and unambiguous words what medication was to be given to which patient, when, how, how much and so on. A medication container would tell the person holding it what its name is, what the appropriate dose is, how it should be used, and what the consequences will be if it is used in any of a variety of improper ways. And it would say all this in multiple ways, clearly and unambiguously, as if on the assumption that the person holding it was blind, stupid, and ignorant.

It is an unfortunate fact that the whole process, from the writing of a prescription to the preparation of the dose, to the administration of the medication, is full of problems stemming from appalling handwriting and ambiguous abbreviations, poorly designed packaging, and non-standard labeling. The gruesome catalog of Medication Errors presented by Davis and Cohen (2) demonstrates the effect of the absence of a controlled vocabulary (3), coupled with an absolute and enforced rejection of deviations from it for everyone involved.

The Mental Act of God (MAOG)

Should people, the instigators, be blamed for their errors? Should they be held responsible? Blame implies that incipient errors can be perceived by the actor before they are executed, and voluntarily controlled to prevent their execution. Responsibility implies that consequences arise because of flaws in behavior.

An Act of God has been defined as: "In law; a direct, sudden, and irresistible action of natural forces, such as could not humanly have been foreseen or prevented." *The American College Dictionary*; and as: "Operation of uncontrollable natural forces." Concise Oxford Dictionary.

Errors, to the extent that we have data, are equally random; the moment when an error will occur cannot be predicted. There is no aura which signals to a perpetrator that an error is about to occur. From the point of view of the person, the error that s/he commits is an MAOG. The actor is the victim of the error; the patient is then the victim of the expression of the error in a medical setting that permitted the error to be completed and produce an injury.

When All Else Fails, Use Failure Mode Analysis

We must accept the fact that various errors will occur and try to prevent or inhibit the translation of the error into an accident. The food and drug administrators and the manufacturers must stop expecting nurses and physicians to use things correctly. Medication packages and medical devices must be subjected to Failure Mode Analysis. We must ask: what incorrect actions can be possible? What will be the result of the incorrect actions? How can we prevent those actions from being completed?

This means that the ways in which each package or device can be misused should be exhaustively tabulated. Then the outcomes of each misuse are identified and evaluated. Those which are unacceptable must be designed out. That is, if a possibility is undesirable, then the possibility must be eliminated. This is like locking the barn door before the horses gallop out; the more usual approach is to use a running-horse detector to lock the doors. For example, the IV system with tubing, bags, Y-ports, and the like can be designed so that a prefilled syringe which is supposed to be injected into an LVP and used as a drip in dilute form must be incapable of being injected into the arm of a Y-port. This requires, of course, meticulous analysis of even such simple systems as a prefilled syringe or the IV set, and the enforcing of standards industry-wide to provide assurance of incompatibility where it is necessary.

Conclusions

There are few or no pure *medical* errors; There are many errors that occur in medical settings. Those that are not prevented from running their courses lead to accidents. These are the ones which come to our attention.

Many of these errors stem from the absence of a controlled and mandatory vocabulary for use in the medical setting. Such errors could be eliminated.

Since not all errors can be prevented, it is necessary to reduce the consequences of the expression of error in the medical setting. Failure mode analysis is the appropriate tool.

Information must be gathered on those errors that do not lead to reportable events. Such data are needed, if we are to predict what kinds of incorrect things are likely to be done in the future.

Whether one knows the causes of some errors, whether one can prevent some errors, are not the ultimate issues. The issues are:

- The identification of the modes of errors in medical settings;
- The prediction of the expression of those errors;
- The use of training and design to improve self-detection;
- The interdiction of their transformation into accidents

References

Adams, J. A., 1982. Issues in human reliability, *Human Factors*, 24:1, 1-10.

Altman, J. W., 1967. Classification of human error. In: *Symposium on reliability of human performance in work*, W. B. Askren (Ed.). 1966 Annual Convention of the American Psychological Association. AMRL-TR 67-88.

Berliner, C., Angel, D., and Shearer, J. W. , 1964. *Behaviors, measures and instruments for performance evaluation in simulated environments*, Symposium and Workshop on the Quantification of Human Performance, Albuquerque, New Mexico.

Embrey, D. E., Humphreys, P., Rosa, E. A., Kirwan, B., and Rea, K., 1984. SLIM-MAUD; An approach to assessing human error probabilities using structured expert judgement,Vols. I & II. NUREG/CR-3518, Washington, D. C.

Freud, S., *The Psychopathology of Everyday Life*, New York, Macmillan Co. trans. from the 4th Ed.

Hall, R. E., Fragola, J. R. and Wreathall, J., 1982. Post-event human decision errors: Operator Action Tree/Time Reliability correlation, NUREG/CR-3010, Washington, D. C.

Hannemen, G. W., and Spurgin, A. J., 1984. Systematic human action reliability procedure (SHARP), EPRI-NP-3583, Palo Alto, Ca.

Kollarits, J., 1937. Beobachtungen, uber dyspraxien (Fehlhandlungen). *Archiv Fur Die Gesamte Psychologie*, 99, 305-399.

Norman, D.A., 1981. Categorization of action slips. *Psych. Rev.*, 88, 1-15.

Phillips, L. D., Humphreys, P. and Embrey, D. E., 1983. A socio-technical approach to assessing human reliability, TR-83-4, ORNL.

Rasmussen, J., 1980. Notes on human error analysis and prediction. In: Postolakes, G., Garriga, S., and Volta, G. (Eds.) *Synthesis and Analysis Methods for Safety and Reliability Studies*, Plenum. N.Y.

Rasmussen, J., 1981. Human errors. A taxonomy for describing human malfunction in industrial installations, RISO-M-2304.

Reason, J. T., 1977. Skill and error in everyday life, In: *Adult Learning*, M. Howe, Ed., London, Wiley.

Sellen, A. J., 1983. The frequency and distribution of errors produced under time stress, B.Sc. diss., Dep't. of Psych., Univ. of Tor.

Sellen, A.J. and Senders, J.W., 1985. At least some errors are random (Freud was wrong), NASA/Univ. 21st Ann. Conf. on Man. Cont., The Ohio St. Univ., Columbus, Ohio.

Sellen, A.J. 1987, An experimental and theoretical investigation of typing errors, M.A.Sc. diss., Dep't. of Ind.Eng., Univ. Tor.

Senders, J. W., 1983, A Theory of Human Error, IEEE Standards Workshop on Human Factors and Nuclear Safety, Myrtle Beach, S. Carolina.

Senders, J. W., 1981. Human error and human reliability in process control, Engineering Foundation Conference on Chemical Process Control, Sea Island, GA, 1981

Senders, J.W., N. P. Moray, A. Smiley, A. J. Sellen, 1986. Cognitive interaction etc, AECB

Sheridan, T. B., 1980. Errors in nuclear power plants, *Technology Review*, vol x, 22-33

Sheridan, T. B., 1983. Measuring, modelling, and augmenting reliability of HO-machine system, *Automatica*, Vol. 19, No. 6, 637-645

Spearman, C.E., The Origin of Error, *Journal of Gen. Psych.*, 1928, 1, 29-53

Siegel, A. I. and Wolf, J. J., 1967. *Man-machine simulation models: performance and psychological interaction*, Wiley, New York.

Swain, A. D. and Guttmann, H. E., 1982. *Handbook of human reliabilityanalysis with emphasis on nuclear power plant applications*, NUREG/CR-1278, Washington, D. C.

Recommended Readings

Senders, J. and M. Cohen, *Near Misses and Real Accidents*, Unpublished survey of nurses' errors, 1992. A questionnaire relating to recalled medication accidents and near misses was filled out by a small sample of nurses. Of 25 who responded one way or the other to the relevant question, only 1 recalled having actually administered an incorrect syringe to a patient; 10 recalled having almost done so, but detected the error before it had been translated into an accident. More data of this kind will be collected and analyzed.

Davis, N. and M. Cohen, *Medication Errors: causes and prevention*, N.M. Davis Assoc., Huntingdon Valley, PA, 1983. This is a catalog of 'errors' submitted over the years to the journal, Hospital Pharmacy, and a discussion and analysis of the various kinds which occur in medical settings. It is a must for anyone involved in the prescription, preparation, and administration of medications.

Davis, N., *Medical Abbreviations: 7000 conveniences at the expense of communications and safety*, N.M. Davis Assoc., Huntingdon Valley, PA, 1988. The title says it all. It is simultaneously a source of information about what various abbreviations (may) mean and an admonition never to use them.

Senders, J. and N. Moray, *Human Error: cause, prediction, and reduction*, Lawrence Erlbaum Associates, Hillsdale, NJ 1991. This volume is a synthesis of the thoughts of 22 scientists in various fields about the nature and source of human error. Its purpose is to stimulate thought and research on the topic.

Reason, J., *Human Error*, Cambridge Univ. Press, 1990. This is a mixture of theory and practicality. Reason surveys the work of others in the field and draws from his own experiments to arrive at a comprehensive overview of human error for behavioral scientists and for those interested in application to real world problems.

Sellen, A., *Mechanisms of Human Error and Human Error Detection;* unpublished PhD Dissertation, Univ. of California at San Diego, 1990. Available from Dissertation Abstracts, Ann Arbor, MI

*Speech delivered at: The American Society of Hospital Pharmacists Annual Meeting Washington, D.C. 2 June, 1992
Theory and Analysis of Typical Errors In A Medical Setting.

John W. Senders

About the Editor

After being thrown out of Antioch College in 1938, John Senders retreated in disgrace to Harvard. There he completed an AB in Experimental Psychology while working on the side as Production Manager of General Controls Co. in Boston. By the time he graduated in 1948 he had become Chief Electronics Engineer, designing automatic control systems and other gadgetry for a variety of industries.

His early interest in aviation (he first flew as a passenger in 1928 and last flew as a pilot in 1988) led him by a circuitous route to the Aero Medical Research Laboratory of the US Air Force in 1950. After five years there and one year as Head of Psychology at the Arctic Aero Medical Laboratory in Fairbanks, Alaska, he returned to industry and established a Human Factors Research group at Minneapolis Honeywell Corporation. In 1962 he accepted an invitation to join JCR Licklider at Bolt, Beranek and Newman in Cambridge, Mass., where he was Principal Scientist and Consultant through 1972. This appointment accidentally brought him to the psychology faculty of Brandeis University as Lecturer and Senior Research Associate in Psychology, 1965-1972. He also fitted in a term as Senior Lecturer in Mechanical Engineering at MIT in 1966-1967.

He was invited to the University of Toronto as Visiting Professor of Industrial Engineering in 1973 and continued as Professor. He retired from Toronto (then mandated at age 65) in 1985 and continued at the University of Maine, at Orono, as Professor of Mechanical Engineering and Experimental Psychology, 1981-1990. He returned to Toronto in 1994. In 1996 he became Lecturer, then Adjunct Professor of Law at the Osgood Hall School of Law at York University teaching his own course: "Intellectual Property Law and Cognitive Science". In 2003-4 he was Professor of Safety Science in the Department of Anesthesiology and Critical Care at the Medical School of University of Miami. In 2006 he was appointed a James Marsh Professor-at-Large at the University of Vermont. He has been an active consultant since 1960 in matters of trademarks, medical safety, human error, etc.

In 1980 he and Ann Crichton-Harris organized and ran the 1st Clambake Conference on the Nature and Source of Human Error at Columbia Falls, Maine. In 1983, with Professor Neville Moray, he organized and ran the 2nd Clambake Conference on the Nature and Source of Human Error at the Rockefeller Foundation's Villa Serbelloni at Lake Como in Italy.

In 1999 John W. Senders co-founded the Institute for Safe Medication Practices—Canada.

.

www.ingramcontent.com/pod-product-compliance
Lightning Source LLC
Chambersburg PA
CBHW050451290526
45786CB00006B/2254